Spacious Dreams

WITHDRAWN

Spacious Dreams

THE FIRST WAVE
OF ASIAN IMMIGRATION

Ronald Takaki, 1939-

PROFESSOR OF ETHNIC STUDIES
THE UNIVERSITY OF CALIFORNIA AT BERKELEY

Adapted by Rebecca Stefoff

Chelsea House Publishers

New York *Philadelphia*

On the cover Chinese immigrants cross the Pacific to America aboard a steamship during the late 1800s.

Chelsea House Publishers

EDITORIAL DIRECTOR   Richard Rennert
EXECUTIVE MANAGING EDITOR   Karyn Gullen Browne
EXECUTIVE EDITOR   Sean Dolan
COPY CHIEF   Robin James
PICTURE EDITOR   Adrian G. Allen
ART DIRECTOR   Robert Mitchell
MANUFACTURING DIRECTOR   Gerald Levine
PRODUCTION COORDINATOR   Marie Claire Cebrián-Ume

The Asian American Experience

SENIOR EDITOR   Jake Goldberg
SERIES DESIGN   Marjorie Zaum

Staff for *Spacious Dreams*
COPY EDITOR   Laura Petermann
EDITORIAL ASSISTANT   Kelsey Goss
PICTURE RESEARCHER   Wendy P. Wills

Adapted and reprinted from *Strangers from a Different Shore,*
© 1989 by Ronald Takaki, by arrangement with the author and
Little Brown and Company, Inc.

First Printing
1 3 5 7 9 8 6 4 2
Library of Congress Cataloging-in-Publication Data
Takaki, Ronald T., 1939–
   Spacious dreams: the first wave of Asian immigration / Ronald
Takaki; introductory essay by Ronald Takaki.
      p. cm.—(The Asian American experience)
   Includes bibliographical references and index.
Summary: A history of the first wave of Asian immigration in America.
ISBN 0-7910-2176-9
      0-7910-2276-5 (pbk.)
   I. Asian Americans—History—Juvenile literature. 2. Asia—Emigra-
tion and immigration— History—Juvenile literature. 3. United States—
Emigration and immigration—History—Juvenile literature. [I. Asian
Americans—History. 2. United States—Emigration and immigration—
History.] I. Title. II. Series: Asian American experience (New York,N.Y.)
E184.O6T34 1993   93-18902
304.8'7305—dc20   CIP
                                                                   AC

Contents

A group of Japanese women, field workers on a
Hawaiian sugar cane plantation.

AS A CHILD IN HAWAII, I GREW UP IN A MULTICULTURAL corner of America. My own family had roots in Japan and China.

Grandfather Kasuke Okawa arrived in Hawaii in 1866, and my father, Toshio Takaki, came as a 13-year-old boy in 1918. My stepfather, Koon Keu Young, sailed from China to the islands when he was a teenager.

My neighbors were Japanese, Chinese, Hawaiian, Filipino, Portuguese, and Korean. Behind my house, Alice Liu and her friends played the traditional Chinese game of mahjongg late into the night, the clicking of the tiles lulling me to sleep.

Next to us the Miuras flew billowing and colorful carp kites on Japanese boy's day. I heard voices with different accents, different languages, and saw children of different colors.

Together we went barefoot to school and played games like baseball and *jan ken po*. We spoke "pidgin English," a melodious language of the streets and community. "Hey, da kind tako ono, you know," we would say, combining English, Japanese, and Hawaiian. "This octopus is delicious." Racially and culturally diverse, we all thought of ourselves as Americans.

But we did not know why families representing such an array of nationalities from different shores were living together and sharing their cultures and a common language. Our teachers and textbooks did not explain the diversity of our community or the sources of our unity.

After graduation from high school, I attended a college in a midwestern town where I found myself invited to "dinners for foreign students" sponsored by local churches and clubs like the Rotary. I politely tried to explain to my kind hosts that I was not a "foreign student." My fellow students and even my professors would ask me how long I had been in America and where I had learned to speak English. "In this country," I would reply. And sometimes I would add: "I was born in America, and my family has been here for three generations."

Asian Americans have been here for over 150 years. They are diverse, coming originally from countries such as China, Japan, Korea, the Philippines, India, Vietnam, Laos, and Cambodia. Many of them live in Chinatowns, the colorful streets filled with sidewalk vegetable stands and crowds of people carrying shopping bags; their communities are also called Little Tokyo, Koreatown, and Little Saigon. Asian Americans work in hot kitchens and bus tables in restaurants with elegant names like Jade Pagoda and Bombay Spice. In garment factories, Chinese and Korean women hunch over whirling sewing machines, their babies sleeping nearby on blankets. In the Silicon Valley of California, rows and rows of Vietnamese and Laotian women serve as the eyes and hands of production assembly lines for computer chip industries. Tough Chinese gang members strut on Grant Avenue in San Francisco and Canal Street in New York's Chinatown. In La Crosse, Wisconsin, Hmong refugees from Laos, now dependent on welfare, sit and stare at the snowdrifts outside their windows. Asian American engineers do complex research in the laboratories of the high-technology industries along

Route 128 in Massachusetts. Asian Americans seem to be everywhere on university campuses.

Today, Asian Americans belong to the fastest growing ethnic group in the United States. Kept out of the United States by immigration restriction laws in the 19th and early 20th centuries, Asians have recently been coming again to America. The 1965 immigration act reopened the gates to immigrants from Asia, allowing 20,000 immigrants from each country to enter every year. In the early 1990s, half of all immigrants entering annually are Asian.

The growth of the Asian-American population has been dramatic: In 1960, there were only 877,934 Asians in the United States, representing a mere one half of 1% of the American people. Thirty years later, they numbered about seven million or 3% of the population. They included 1,645,000 Chinese, 1,400,000 Filipinos, 845,000 Japanese, 815,000 Asian Indians, 800,000 Koreans, 614,000 Vietnamese, 150,000 Laotians, 147,000 Cambodians, and 90,000 Hmong. By the year 2000, Asian Americans will probably represent 4% of the total United States population. In California, Asian Americans already make up 10% of the state's inhabitants, compared with 7.5% for African Americans.

Yet very little is known about Asian Americans and their history. Many existing history books give Asian Americans only passing notice—or overlook them entirely. "When one hears Americans tell of the immigrants who built this nation," Congressman Norman Mineta of California observed, "one is often led to believe that all our forebearers came from Europe. When one hears stories about the pioneers going West to shape the land, the Asian immigrant is rarely mentioned."

Indeed, many history books have equated "American" with "white" or "European" in origin. In his prize-winning study, *The Uprooted*, Harvard historian Oscar Handlin presented—to use the book's subtitle—"the Epic Story of the Great Migrations that Made the American People." But Handlin's "epic story" completely left out the "uprooted" from lands across the Pacific Ocean and the "great migrations" from Asia that also helped to make "the American people." As Americans, we have origins in Europe, the Americas, Africa, and also Asia.

We need to include Asians in the history of America. How and why, we ask in this series, were the experiences of these various groups—Chinese, Japanese, Korean, Filipino, Asian Indian, and Southeast Asian—similar to and different from each other? Comparing the experiences of different nationalities can help us see what events were particular to a group and also highlight the experiences they all shared.

Why did Asian immigrants leave everything they knew and loved to come to a strange world so far away? They were "pushed" by hardships in the homelands and "pulled" by demands for their labor in Canada, Brazil, and especially the United States. But what were their own fierce dreams— from the first enterprising Chinese miners of the 1850s in search of "Gold Mountain" to the recent refugees fleeing frantically on helicopters and leaking boats from the ravages of war in Vietnam?

Besides their points of origin, we need to examine the experiences of Asian Americans in different geographical regions, especially Hawaii compared with the mainland. The time of arrival also shaped their lives and communities. About one million people entered the United States between the California gold rush of 1849 and the 1924 immigration act that cut off the flow of peoples from Asian countries. After a break of some 40 years, a second group numbering about four million came between 1965 and 1990. How do we compare the two waves of Asian immigration?

To answer our questions in these volumes, we must study Asian Americans as men and women with minds, wills, and voices. By "voices" we mean their own words and stories as told in their oral histories, conversations, speeches, and songs as well as their own writings—diaries, letters, newspapers, novels, and poems. We need to know the ordinary people.

So much of history has been the story of kings and elites, as if the "little people" were invisible and voiceless. An Asian American told an interviewer: "I am a second generation Korean American without any achievements in life and I have no education. What is it you want to hear from me? My life is not worth telling to anyone." Similarly, a Chinese immigrant said: "You know, it seems to me there's no use in me telling you all this! I was just a simple worker, a farm worker around here. My story is not going to interest anybody." But others realize they are worthy of attention. "What is it you want to know?" an old Filipino immigrant asked a researcher. "Talk about history. What's that . . . ah, the story of my life . . . and how people lived with each other in my time."

Their stories can enable us to understand Asians as actors in the making of history and as people entitled to dignity. "I hope this survey do a lot of good for Chinese people," a Chinese man told an interviewer from Stanford University in the 1920s. "Make American people realize that Chinese people are humans. I think very few American people really know anything about Chinese." Elderly Asians want the younger generations to know about their experiences. "Our stories should be listened to by many young people," said a 91-year-old retired Japanese plantation laborer. "It's for their sake. We really had a hard time, you know."

The stories of Asian immigrations belong to our country's history. They need to be recorded in our history books, for they reflect the making of America as a nation of immigrants, as a place where men and women came to find a new beginning. At first, many Asian immigrants—probably most of them—saw themselves as sojourners, or temporary migrants. Like many European immigrants such as the Italians and Greeks, they came to America thinking they would be here only a short time. They had left their wives and children behind in their homelands. Their plan was to work here for a few years and then return home with money. But, after their arrival, many found themselves staying. They became settlers instead of remaining sojourners. Bringing their families to their adopted country, they began putting down new roots in America.

But, coming here from Asia, many of America's immigrants found they were not allowed to feel at home in the United States. Even their grandchildren and great-grandchildren still find they are not viewed and accepted as Americans. "We feel that we're a guest in someone else's house," said third generation Ron Wakabayashi, National

Director of the Japanese American Citizens League, "that we can never really relax and put our feet on the table."

Behind Wakabayashi's complaint is the question: Why have Asian Americans been considered outsiders? America's immigrants from Pacific shores found they were forced to remain strangers in the new land. Their experiences here were profoundly different from the experiences of European immigrants. Asian immigrants had qualities they could not change or hide—the shape of their eyes, the color of their hair, the complexion of their skins. They were subjected not only to cultural and ethnic prejudice but also to racism. Unlike the Irish and other groups from Europe, Asian immigrants were not treated as individuals but as members of a group with distinctive physical characteristics. Regardless of their personal merits, they sadly discovered, they could not gain acceptance in the larger society.

Unlike European immigrants, Asians were victimized by laws and policies that discriminated on the basis of race. The Chinese Exclusion Act of 1882 barred the Chinese from coming to America because they were Chinese. The National Origins Act of 1924 totally prohibited Japanese immigration.

The laws determined not only who could come to America but also who could become citizens. Decades before Asian immigration began, the United States had already defined the complexion of its citizens: the Naturalization Law of 1790 had specified that naturalized citizenship was to be reserved for "whites." This law remained in effect until 1952. Unlike white ethnic immigrants from countries like Ireland, Asian immigrants were denied citizenship and also the right to vote.

But America also had an opposing tradition and vision, springing from the reality of racial and cultural "diversity." Ours has been, as Walt Whitman celebrated so lyrically, "a teeming Nation of nations" composed of a "vast, surging, hopeful army of workers," a new society where all should be welcomed, "Chinese, Irish, German,—all, all, without exceptions." In the early 20th century, a Japanese immigrant described in poetry a lesson that had been learned by farm laborers of different nationalities—Japanese, Filipino, Mexican, and Asian Indian:

> *People harvesting*
> *Work together unaware*
> *Of racial problems.*

A Filipino immigrant laborer in California expressed a similar hope and understanding. America was, Macario Bulosan told his brother Carlos, "not a land of one race or one class of men" but "a new world" of respect and unconditional opportunities for all who toiled and suffered from oppression, from "the first Indian that offered peace in Manhattan to the last Filipino pea pickers." Asian immigrants came here, as one of them expressed it, searching for "a door into America" and seeking "to build a new life with untried materials." He asked: "Would it be possible for an immigrant like me to become a part of the American dream?"

This series invites students to learn how Asian Americans belong to the larger story of the rich multicultural mosaic called the United States of America.

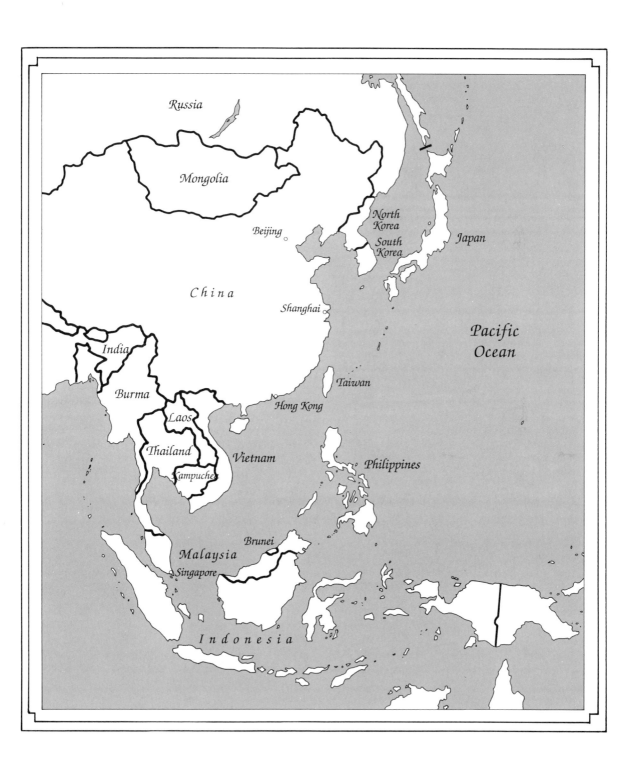

A Japanese woman loads sugar cane onto a wagon. Asian workers provided the labor that made sugar "king" on Hawaii's hugely profitable plantations.

Chapter One

"Get Labor First"

GLANCING OVER THEIR SHOULDERS AS THEY LABORED in the hot sugar mill, the Chinese men saw a white man standing nearby. He was a *haole*, the Hawaiian word for a foreigner or outsider, a Caucasian. The workers had a white boss, but this *haole* was a stranger. What was he doing there? And what were these Chinese men doing in Hawaii, half an ocean away from their homeland?

The year was 1835. A handful of Chinese lived and worked in Kauai, one of the islands of the Hawaiian kingdom. Just half a century earlier the Hawaiian islands had been unknown to both China and the Western world. But in 1778 Captain James Cook, exploring the Pacific Ocean for Britain, had bumped into the island chain. As soon as word of Cook's "discovery" spread, European and American traders and missionaries hurried to Hawaii. Western ships began making trading voyages between Hawaii and Asia. They carried sandalwood, a fragrant Hawaiian wood, to China, where it was greatly prized. Chinese men worked as sailors on some of the ships, and a few of these men stayed in Hawaii. On Kauai, where sugar cane grew wild, they found work at the sugar mill. They knew about making sugar; for centuries the Chinese had been turning the juice of the sugar cane into sweet crystals.

The *haole* newcomer who visited the sugar mill that day in 1835 was William Hooper, a young man from Boston. His mission was to clear land, plant sugar cane, and start the first sugar plantation in Hawaii. After his visit to the sugar mill, he informed his employer, the Honolulu trading firm of Ladd and Company, that the Chinese laborers worked six days

Hawaiians offer hospitality to British explorer James Cook and his officers. Cook landed in Hawaii—which he called the Sandwich Islands—in 1778, and soon European and American ships were making regular stops there.

a week. "They have to work *all* the time," he wrote, "and no regard is paid to their complaints for food, etc., etc. Slavery is nothing compared to it."

A few months later, Hooper began setting up his plantation. He knew he had to get labor first of all, so he hired 25 Hawaiians. He agreed to pay each of them $2 a month. Hooper's second step was to measure out a 12-acre area for his plantation. Two days later the workers arrived at sunrise. They began work after breakfast, and by the end of the day they had cleared the grass from two acres.

About a year later, in September 1836, Hooper proudly listed his accomplishments. He had begun growing sugar cane on 25 acres of land, and he had built a sugar mill. His Hawaiian workers lived on the plantation and were paid with coupons—pieces of cardboard on which Hooper had written various amounts, such as "25 Cents" or "50 Cents." With these coupons the workers could "buy" goods at the plantation store.

Hooper had made progress, but he was not satisfied with his Hawaiian workers. He complained that they were hard to discipline. They did not always show up for work on time or work as hard as he expected. In a letter to Ladd and Company, he declared that the Hawaiian natives "are alas, children, boys, and always will be." Hooper recommended getting half a dozen Chinese laborers. The Chinese, he said, would work more diligently than the Hawaiians.

Shortly after this Hooper hired some Chinese men. He assigned them to work in the mill, while the Hawaiians labored in the fields. In April 1838 he informed his company that a large building had been constructed for the "Chinamen" to live in. He wrote, "They are highly pleased, and by their fixtures on doors I should suppose they intend to spend their days in it." Early the next year Hooper ordered a supply of rice, the staple food of the Chinese.

To Hooper's dismay, the arrival of the Chinese did not mean the end of his labor troubles. New troubles arose as the workers, both Hawaiian and Chinese, found ways to resist management. For example, they devised a clever method of getting goods from the company store. They had learned to read and write from a young schoolmaster in the village, and some of them used their new skills to make artful reproductions of Hooper's handwritten coupons. The counterfeit coupons, said a neighbor, were "so strikingly like the original, imitating the signatures with scrupulous exactness, that it was

Bostonian William Hooper
started the first sugar
plantation in Hawaii and
imported Chinese laborers to
work on it. The Chinese, he
reported, worked harder
than slaves.

some time before the fraud was detected." Both Hawaiians and Chinese tried their hand at counterfeiting the coupons.

Determined to outwit the wily forgers, Hooper asked Ladd and Company to have scrip, or paper money, printed in Boston. In a letter to the printer, the company said: "If the ground work is fine waved lines, or delicate net work, and the border highly wrought, we doubt if we shall be troubled with counterfeits from the Chinese or any other source."

Hooper was pleased with the printed scrip, but he did not stay on the plantation to see how well it worked. He returned to Boston in 1839, leaving behind him a place that had been transformed from lush wilderness into ordered rows of cane. In 1837–38 he had shipped 30 tons of sugar to Honolulu. From this small but significant beginning, sugar was to grow into a large industry—an industry that would need a steady supply of workers from Asia.

The sugar plantations of Hawaii were not the only places that needed Asian immigrant laborers. International events drew workers from Asia to the American mainland as well. In 1848, after a war with Mexico, the United States gained control of a region that had been part of Mexico for centuries: California and the American Southwest. Surveying this new U.S. territory, America's leaders wondered how to make it productive and profitable. A government official named Aaron H. Palmer shared his ideas with Congress. He recommended that the United States should put a fleet of steamships in the Pacific Ocean and make San Francisco into the center of American trade with China. Connected by railroad to the Atlantic states, San Francisco would become America's gateway to Asia, the "great emporium of our commerce on the Pacific." And, Palmer added, Chinese laborers should be imported to build the transcontinental railroad and to farm the fertile lands of California. "No people in all the East are so well adapted for clearing wild lands and raising every species of agricultural product . . . as the Chinese," Palmer wrote.

Planter William Hooper and economic planner Aaron Palmer shared a view of the world that was common among white Americans of the time. Like the Pilgrims before them, they felt it was wrong to let the land "lie in waste." Their vision of Chinese workers growing sugar cane in Hawaii and building railroads across the West reflected an important theme of American history. From the very beginning, the English settlers in America had a mission: to remake the new world in their own image, to turn it from an idle wilderness into a busy, settled landscape.

During the 19th century, the United States expanded westward to the Pacific frontier. By 1848 the United States was poised on the western edge of the continent, ready to advance its market civilization into Asia. Five years later, Commodore Matthew C. Perry of the U.S. Navy sailed his warships into a Japanese harbor and forced Japan at cannon point to open its doors to American "friendship" and "commerce."

The United States did not simply want to trade with the Pacific world; it wanted its own Pacific outposts. In 1898 the United States took possession of both Hawaii and the Philippine Islands. By the end of the 19th century, America's grip reached all the way across the vast Pacific Ocean.

It would take hard work to turn Hawaii into a fruitful plantation colony and the Western frontier into a hub of economic development. Much of that work was done by "strangers from a different shore"—from China and also from Japan, Korea, the Philippines, and India.

"Get labor first," sugar planters in Hawaii said. With enough workers they would make profits, which could be used to buy more land, plant more sugar, and hire more workers. During the second half of the 19th century, the planters made sugar "king" in Hawaii. They were American businessmen and sons of American missionaries who turned the island kingdom into an economic colony of the United States.

The planters helped arrange for the 1875 Reciprocity Treaty between the governments of Hawaii and the United States. This treaty permitted the island kingdom to sell sugar to the United States without paying duties, or import taxes. Investments in cane growing became a "mania," and the production of sugar jumped from 9,392 tons in 1870 to nearly 300,000 tons in 1900. Between 1875 and 1910, the amount of land cultivated for cane plantations multiplied nearly 18 times, from 12,000 acres to 214,000 acres. Sugar was Hawaii's most important export. In 1897, a year before the United States took possession of the islands, sugar exports accounted for $15 million out of a total of $16 million in exports.

The growth of the sugar industry depended upon labor for the plantations. The planters, however, did not want to rely on Hawaiian labor. Few native workers were available because the Hawaiian population had been dropping sharply for several decades, largely due to diseases brought there by whites. In addition, Hawaiian workers were not easily disciplined. They could not be threatened with the loss of their jobs because they could survive by farming and fishing.

So the planters followed the suggestion that William Hooper had made in the 1830s. They turned to Chinese labor. In 1850 they founded the Royal Hawaiian Agricultural Society to bring workers from China. Two years later, after the arrival of the first Chinese laborers, the president of the Society predicted: "We shall find Coolie labor to be far more certain, systematic, and economic than that of the native. They are prompt at the call of the bell, steady in their work, quick to learn, and will accomplish more."

The Chinese were not the only group brought to Hawaii to work in the cane fields. In the years to come the planters would look all over the world, including Europe, for workers. But they looked mainly to Asia.

Planters obtained their workers from labor suppliers, Honolulu firms such as Castle and Cooke or Theo. H. Davies and Company. They sent these suppliers lists of the things they needed. In 1890, the Davies Company wrote to the manager of the Laupahoehoe Plantation, saying that the company had received the manager's order for:

bonemeal

canvas

Japanese laborers

macaroni

a Chinaman

Another letter from the Davies Company confirmed an order that included: "LABORERS. We will book your order for 75 Japanese to come as soon as possible" and "MULES & HORSES." A letter from H. Hackfield and Company to the Grove Farm Plantation on Kauai listed orders alphabetically:

Fertilizer

Filipinos

When ordering laborers, the planters were careful to build a work force from many different ethnic backgrounds. They did this not because they prized ethnic diversity for its own sake but because it was easier for them to control a work force made up of different nationalities. In the 1850s, the planters used the hard-working Chinese to set an "example" for the Hawaiian workers. Managers hoped the Hawaiians would be "naturally jealous" of the foreigners and "ambitious" to outdo them. They encouraged the Chinese to call the native workers "wahine! wahine!"—Hawaiian for "women! women!"

At first the planters were successful in pitting the Chinese against the Hawaiian workers. The Chinese worked hard, as the planters had expected. But the planters' strategy later backfired. They became dependent upon the Chinese laborers, who soon outnumbered the Hawaiians. The planters learned, however, that they could not set the Chinese against one another as they had pitted the Chinese against the Hawaiians. In addition, the Chinese eventually wanted higher wages. The planters needed to find a new source of workers they could use to control the Chinese.

They turned to Portuguese and then to Japanese workers. The Japanese newcomers, in particular, would work more cheaply than the Chinese. The Chinese thus had to accept lower wages or lose their jobs. This made the planters happy, and by the 1890s, the islands' work force consisted mostly of Japanese. So the planters recruited Chinese laborers to mix with the Japanese. They encouraged the Chinese and Japanese to view each other as rivals. By setting the two groups against one another, the planters made each group work harder and obey orders more readily.

The planters used ethnic diversity to break strikes and repress unions. On plantations where the workers were mostly from the same country, laborers cooperated in efforts to raise their pay or improve their working conditions. But workers of different nationalities found it harder to communicate, and in some cases there were ethnic rivalries between them. Members of different groups were less likely to form unions or go on strike together for better pay. One plantation manager advised his fellow planters to employ as many different nationalities as possible to "offset" the power of any one group.

Bluntly stating the planters' divide-and-rule strategy, another manager advised, "Keep a variety of laborers . . . for there are few, if any, cases of Japs, Chinese, and Portuguese entering into a strike as a unit." In 1896 the labor supplier

An early labor camp on a Hawaiian plantation. Some women worked in the fields, but most performed other jobs, such as laundering, cooking, and sewing.

H. Hackfield and Company wrote a confidential letter to a planter saying, "Regarding the proportion of Chinese and Japanese laborers we beg to advise, that the Hawaiian Sugar Planters' Association and the Bureau of Immigration have agreed upon 2/3rd of the former and 1/3rd of the latter. For your *private* information we mention, that the reason for this increasing the percentage of the Chinese laborers is due to the desire of breaking up the preponderance of the Japanese element."

After Hawaii was annexed, or added to the United States, laws that had been passed to keep Chinese from immigrating to the U.S. mainland now applied to the islands. Planters could no longer import Chinese laborers. Worried that the "Japs" were "getting too numerous," the planters looked for new sources of labor. Their favorite method of dividing the work force was to split it "about equally between two Oriental nationalities," so they turned to Korea. They planned to pit Korean workers against the "excess of Japanese."

Korean workers were introduced to the plantations in 1903. At that time Japan was preparing to extend its rule over Korea, and Japanese and Koreans were hostile to one another. The planters could be pretty sure that the Koreans were "not likely to combine with the Japanese at any attempt at strikes." One planter, angry at his Japanese workers for demanding higher wages, asked a labor company to send him a shipment of Korean workers soon, saying, "In our opinion, it would be advisable, as soon as circumstances permit, to get a large number of Koreans in the country . . . and drive the Japs out."

Just as the Chinese labor supply had been cut off by U.S. immigration laws, the Korean labor supply ended when the government of Korea banned emigration to Hawaii in 1905. Once again the planters had to find a new source of workers to till the cane fields and labor in the sugar mills. This time they turned to the Philippines.

The first Filipino laborers arrived on the plantations in 1906. A labor recruiter displayed these workers on the dock in Honolulu, promising that if the Filipino were treated right, he would be a "first-class laborer," "possibly not as good as the Chinaman or the Jap, but steady, faithful and willing to do his best for any boss for whom he has a liking."

Soon the planters were importing massive numbers of Filipino workers. Agreements between Japan and the United States had cut the flow of Japanese migrants. Furthermore, Japanese laborers were unpopular with the sugar planters because in 1909 they had gone on strike. During the strike, the Hawaiian Sugar Planters' Association reported that several hundred Filipino laborers were on their way to Hawaii: "It may be too soon to say that the Jap is to be supplanted, but it is certainly in order to take steps to clip his wings."

The Filipinos, like the Chinese and Koreans, were used by the planters to control and discipline the Japanese workers. One planter, complaining that his Japanese workers were demanding higher wages, wrote to a labor company, "If possible for you to arrange it I should very much like to get say 25 new Filipinos to put into our day gang. . . . In this way perhaps we can stir the Japs a bit." Twenty days later he wrote again, saying he was very pleased to receive the shipment of 30 Filipinos and hoped he could use them to bring the Japanese workers to "their senses."

Half a century after the first cane plantation was founded, Hawaii's sugar planters were drawing large numbers of workers from Asian shores. By using ethnic diversity as a tool for controlling their laborers, they were laying the foundation of a multicultural society in the islands.

Like the planters in Hawaii, businessmen in the United States knew they needed to "get labor first." Steamships crossed the seas, bringing Asia to America's Pacific "door" and giving American employers access to the "unnumbered millions" of workers in Asia. California, in particular, needed workers.

In an 1869 magazine article called "Our Manufacturing Era," a writer named Henry Robinson described California's enormous economic potential. California had every variety of climate and soil, a nearly completed railroad, an abundance of fuel and water power, markets in Asia and the Pacific, and an unlimited supply of low-wage labor from

An illustration published in a London newspaper in 1876 shows Chinese immigrants aboard the steamship Alaska, *bound for San Francisco. To European eyes, the clothing and customs of the Chinese seemed exotic and alien.*

China. Robinson claimed that even a lowly job in America would be a step up for an Asian, who would do work that whites had "outgrown." He concluded, "If Chinese labor could be used to develop the industries of California, it would be the height of folly to forbid its entrance to the Golden Gate."

Around the same time, a California farmer stated frankly that he could not get white workers to do stoop labor in the fields. "I must employ Chinamen or give up," he said. And San Francisco minister Otis Gibson reported in 1877 that there was a constant demand for Chinese labor all over the Pacific Coast because reliable white labor was not available at wages that employers could afford to pay.

American employers had·a divide-and-control plan like that of the Hawaiian planters. And like the Hawaiian planters, employers on the mainland repeatedly had to find new sources of labor. They started with the Chinese and then turned to other Asian nationalities.

In the middle years of the 19th century, employers used Chinese workers to give low-ranking white workers the hope that someday they would become bosses themselves. Railroad builder Charles Crocker said, "After we got Chinamen to work, we took the more intelligent of the white laborers and made foremen of them. . . . They got a start by controlling Chinese labor on our railroad."

But the Chinese could also be used to make white workers work harder for lower wages. E. L. Godkin of *The Nation* predicted that bosses would use Chinese labor to resist white workers' strikes. If the white workers' demands were too great, the employers had within their reach millions of Chinese "ready to work for small wages." In 1870 a traveler in

From the middle of the 19th century through the first quarter of the 20th century, Asian immigrants poured into the United States to fill the need for labor, especially in California and other western states. Nearly a million Asians came to American shores in this first wave of immigration.

California reported: "In the factories of San Francisco they had none but Irish, paying them three dollars a day in gold. They struck, and demanded four dollars. Immediately their places, numbering three hundred, were supplied by Chinamen at one dollar a day."

The factory owners, bankers, investors, and other leaders of American industry used Chinese laborers to keep the wages of white workers low during periods of economic growth and to prevent strikes by white workers when times grew hard. By importing Chinese workers, the bosses could boost the supply of labor; this drove down the wages of both Chinese and white workers. As a result of these manipulations, the Chinese and white workers naturally resented one another. Racial antagonism kept the working class divided. And because the working class was weak, the employer class remained dominant.

Toward the end of the 19th century, many white Americans thought that there were too many Chinese in the United States. Congress acted on this belief in 1882 by passing a law called the Chinese Exclusion Act, which banned Chinese immigration. The need for labor remained, however, and six years later the first Japanese workers appeared in America: 60 Japanese were brought to Vacaville, California, to pick fruit.

When sugar-beet farming grew into an important agricultural industry in the 1890s, the demand for farm labor rose sharply. By the end of the century, farmers in California complained of tons of fruit and vegetables rotting in the fields because there were no workers to pick the crops. Faced with a labor shortage, more and more farmers hired Japanese laborers. Testifying before a congressional committee in 1907, sugar-beet king John Spreckels said, "If we do not have the Japs to do the field labor, we would be in a bad fix, because you know American labor will not go into the fields."

American farmers saw another advantage in using Japanese labor. "The Japs just drift—we don't have to look out for them," explained an official of the California Fruit Growers' Exchange. "White laborers with families, if we could get them, would be liabilities."

By then, however, growers were facing demands for higher wages from Japanese workers. In 1907, the *California Fruit Grower* complained that "the labor problem" had become "extremely troublesome." Labor was in short supply, and employers had been forced to raise wages. The journal recommended a new source of labor: Asian Indians. A year later, California farmers hired Asian Indians as "a check on the Japanese," paying them 25 cents less a day than they paid

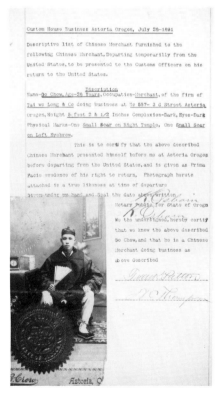

After laws were passed to keep Chinese immigrants from entering the United States, merchants who left the country on business had to prove their identity when they returned. This document allowed merchant Go Chow of Astoria, Oregon, to reenter the United States.

Japanese apple pickers in a California orchard. The skill and strength of Japanese migrant workers and farmers turned barren lands into productive fruit farms and vegetable gardens.

Japanese workers. Shortly after the introduction of the Asian Indian laborers, John Spreckels told a congressional committee that "if it had not been for the large number of these East Indians coming in there . . . we would have had to take all Japs."

During the 1920s, farmers turned to Mexico as their main source of labor. At least 150,000 of California's 200,000 farm laborers were Mexican. An official for the California Fruit Growers' Association praised the Mexican workers. Unlike the Chinese and Japanese, the Mexicans were "not aggressive." Instead they were "amenable to suggestions" and did their work obediently. But the growers were afraid that the flow of Mexican workers would be cut off by the Immigration Act of 1924, so they began to import laborers from the Philippines.

Because the Philippine Islands were U.S. territory, the Immigration Act did not apply to Filipinos, and employers saw the islands as a limitless source of labor. "The Filipinos," reported the *Pacific Rural Press*, "are being rushed in as the Mexicans are being rushed out."

Like the Hawaiian sugar planters, California farmers found that an ethnically diverse labor force gave them greater control over their workers. A member of the State Employment Agency told an interviewer in 1930 how farmers could get the most work out of Japanese and Chinese laborers: "Put a gang of Chinese in one field and a gang of Japanese in the next, and each one works like hell to keep up with or keep ahead of the other."

Noting the presence of Mexican, Chinese, Japanese, Asian Indian, Portuguese, Korean, Puerto Rican, and Filipino farm workers, the California Department of Industrial Rela-

A health inspector examines young Asian men seeking to enter the United States. Immigration procedures were casual at first, but over time rules and regulations were created to govern them.

tions reported that growers preferred to "employ a mixture of laborers of various races, speaking diverse languages, and not accustomed to mingling with each other." With workers of different nationalities, bosses ran less risk of strikes.

The Asian labor migrations to Hawaii and North America were part of the development of the modern world economy. Trading and manufacturing nations, such as the United States, Britain, France, and Spain, were entering the less-developed lands of Asia, Africa, Latin America, and the

Pacific. In their search for raw materials, laborers, and new places to sell their manufactured goods, the Europeans and Americans disrupted economies in these lands and often worsened poverty there. Migrants from the less-developed parts of the world were both "pushed" out of their homelands by poverty and "pulled" to new lives by the desire for work.

Many European immigrants to North America were pushed and pulled by the same forces. But the Asian migrants came from "a different shore." They were a laboring army of "strangers," people of alien origins and appearances. As non-whites, they were allowed to enter as "cheap" laborers, but they were not considered to be future citizens of American society.

Poverty and hard times in Asia were not the only reasons for the Asian migrations to America. There were Asians who experienced the same economic pressures but remained at home. But many Asians left home voluntarily after weighing the possibilities open to them. They made choices about the direction of their lives, and therefore they made history.

The laborers themselves had their own view of their migrations. They did not come across the ocean to fill the orders of businessmen who listed them along with macaroni and fertilizer. Nor did they come to be pitted against workers of other nationalities and to break strikes, or to hold down the wages of white workers, or to be the bottom rank of American society. The Asian migrants had reasons of their own for leaving their homelands. They spoke of their "spacious dreams" and "overblown hopes." What were those dreams and hopes?

A Chinese family. Many families were separated forever when the men migrated to America to seek their fortunes and found themselves unable to return to their homeland.

Chapter Two

To Fragrant Hills and Gold Mountains

MOST CHINESE LABORERS LEFT HOME AS SOJOURNERS, hoping to work in a foreign country and return home rich in three to five years. They gave names to their destinations: *Tan Heung Shan* ("Fragrant Sandalwood Hills") for the Hawaiian Islands and *Gam Saan* ("Gold Mountain") for California. Beginning in the 1840s and 1850s, they left China by the tens of thousands. About 46,000 of them went to Hawaii in the second half of the 19th century, and about 380,000 went to the United States mainland between 1849 and 1930.

The Chinese already had a long history of movement overseas. By the 17th century, there were 10,000 Chinese in Thailand and 20,000 in the Philippines. These migrants had defied the imperial Chinese governments, which from the 14th century on had forbidden Chinese people to travel overseas on pain of death. But the greatest outflow of Chinese occurred in the 19th century. Between 1840 and 1900, an estimated 2.5 million people left China. They went to Hawaii and the United States and also to Canada, Australia, New Zealand, Southeast Asia, the West Indies, South America, and Africa.

Most of the Chinese who came to Hawaii and the United States were from Guangdong province on the south coast of China. They were fleeing a region that was torn by intense conflicts. The city of Canton (now called Guangzhou) was the focus of two wars with Britain—the Opium Wars of 1839–42 and 1856–60—in which China was defeated and forced to allow opium to be sold in Chinese ports. Southern China was also devastated by such wide-ranging peasant rebellions as the Red Turban Rebellion of 1854–64, by fierce ethnic strife over possession of the fertile delta lands, and by class and family feuds within villages. Forced to flee from this violence and turmoil, many Chinese migrants felt "pushed" from their home country. One migrant described this expulsion:

> In a bloody feud between the Chang family and the Oo Shak village we lost our two steady workmen. Eighteen villagers were hired by Oo Shak to fight against the huge Chang family, and in the battle two men lost their lives protecting our pine forests. Our village, Wong Jook Long, had a few resident Changs. After the bloodshed, we were called for our men's lives, and the greedy, impoverished villagers grabbed fields, forest, food and everything, including newborn pigs, for payment. We were left with nothing, and in disillusion we went to Hong Kong to sell ourselves as contract laborers.

But most of the migrants were driven by poverty to seek survival in another country. When China's government was forced to pay large penalties to the Western powers after the Opium Wars, it imposed high taxes on the peasant farmers to raise money for the penalties. Many farmers were unable to pay these taxes, so their land was seized. Displaced from their land, they had no way to make a living.

The hardships were particularly severe in Guangdong province, where the population had increased by 76% in 63 years—from 16 million in 1787 to 28 million in 1850. Floods intensified the problems of overcrowding, poverty, and hunger. Starvation lay behind the emigrating spirit, as one

observer explained in 1852: "The population is extremely dense; the means of subsistence, in ordinary times, are seldom above the demand, and, consequently, the least failure of the rice crop produces wretchedness." One of the migrants gave his own account of the painful events leading to emigration:

A fanciful engraving of a Chinese port, made in 1840, reflects the common 19th-century Western view of China as a quaint, picturesque land. It fails to show the poverty, overcrowding, and famine from which many Chinese peasants suffered.

> There were four in our family, my mother, my father, my sister and me. We lived in a two room house. Our sleeping room and the other served as parlor, kitchen and dining room. We were not rich enough to keep pigs or fowls, otherwise, our small house would have been more than overcrowded.

> How can we live on six baskets of rice which were paid twice a year for my father's duty as a night watchman? Sometimes the peasants have a poor crop then we go hungry. . . . Sometimes we went hungry for days. My mother and me would go over the harvested rice fields of the peasants to pick the grains they dropped. . . . We had only salt and water to eat with the rice.

Learning about the Fragrant Hills and Gold Mountain, many of the younger, more impatient, and more courageous men left their villages for the distant lands. Most of them were married. They were generally illiterate or had very little schooling, but they dreamed of new possibilities for themselves inspired by stories about the fortunes to be made in Hawaii and California.

In 1848, shortly after the discovery of gold at John Sutter's mill in California, a young man in Canton wrote to his brother in Boston. He said, "Good many Americans speak of California. Oh! Very rich country! I hear good many Americans and Europeans go there. Oh! They find gold very quickly, so I hear. . . . I feel as if I should like to go there very much. I think I shall go to California next summer." A witness in China described how letters from Chinese in San Francisco spread the exciting news of the gold rush throughout China, adding that if everyone who dreamed of going to California had been able to afford the trip, whole towns in China would have been emptied.

"Gold Mountain" promised not only gold to be mined but also job opportunities. In the port cities, leaflets distributed by labor brokers announced, "Americans are very rich people. They want the Chinaman to come and make him very welcome. There you will have great pay, large houses, and food and clothing of the finest description. . . . Money is in great plenty and to spare in America." During the 1860s, a Chinese laborer might earn $3 to $5 a month in South China; in California, he could work for the railroad and make $30 a month.

The Chinese who returned to their villages with money they had earned in Hawaii and America added to the excitement. Sixteen-year-old Lee Chew remembered the triumphant return of a Chinese migrant from the "country of the American wizards." With the money he had earned overseas, he bought land as spacious as "four city blocks" and built a palace on it. He also invited his fellow villagers to a grand party where they were served a hundred roasted pigs, along with chickens, ducks, geese, and an abundance of dainties. The young Lee was inspired, eager to go to America himself.

America seemed so beckoning. "After leaving the village," an immigrant said, "I went to Hong Kong and stayed at a *gam saan jong* ['golden mountain firm'] owned by people named Quan. I stayed there ten days to take care of the paper work for passage. At that time all I knew was that *gam saan haak* ['travelers to the golden mountain'] who came back were always rich." A popular Chinese saying of the time promised

Faces filled with mingled hope and uncertainty, Chinese emigrants leave their homeland for the "fragrant sandalwood hills" of Hawaii or the "gold mountain" of California.

41

that if a sojourner could not save a thousand dollars, he would surely get at least eight hundred. But even with only three hundred dollars he could return to China and become "a big, very big gentleman." A folk song expressed the emotions of many *gam saan haak*:

> *In the second reign year of Haamfung [1852], a trip to*
> *   Gold Mountain was made.*
> *With a pillow on my shoulder, I began my perilous journey:*
> *Sailing a boat with bamboo poles across the sea,*
> *Leaving behind wife and sisters in search of money,*
> *No longer lingering with the woman in the bedroom,*
> *No longer paying respect to parents at home.*

But how could poor peasants afford to go to Hawaii and America? The migrants were told they did not need much money to get there. They could go as contract laborers to Hawaii. Under arrangements made by the sugar planters of Hawaii, the migrants could have "free passage" to the islands. They would sign labor agreements to work for a planter for five years. In return they would receive wages, shelter, food, and medical care.

Or they could go to the United States as free laborers under the credit-ticket system. Under this arrangement, a broker would loan money to a migrant to buy his ticket, and the migrant in turn would pay off the loan plus interest out of his earnings in the new country. Chung Kun Ai recalled how his grandfather went into such moneylending as a business venture: "One condition of his loan of $60 was that each borrower was to pay back $120 as soon as he was able to do so. In all, grandfather must have helped 70 young men from our village and nearby villages to migrate to North and South America and also Australia."

Contrary to a popular myth, the Chinese migrants to North America were not "coolies"—laborers who had been kidnapped, forced, or tricked into service and shipped to a foreign country. Thousands of Chinese were taken to Peru and Cuba this way, but the migrants to the United States came voluntarily. Some Chinese paid their own way; probably most of them borrowed the money under the credit-ticket system. "The Chinese emigration to California," reported a British official stationed in Hong Kong in 1853, "was, by and large, free and voluntary." William Speer, who worked as a missionary in San Francisco's Chinatown for decades beginning in the 1850s, never found evidence that Chinese laborers had been brought to America and used as slaves against their will. Such a claim, he insisted, was "a fiction."

The Chinese migration also included merchants—daring businessmen seeking new opportunities for enterprise in foreign lands. One of them was the father of Koon Keu Young, my stepfather. While maintaining his business operations in Guangdong, he went to Hawaii and opened two grocery stores in Honolulu, importing goods and foods from China. He brought two of his sons to Hawaii to run the stores and then returned to China. Koon Keu Young was only 16 years old when he arrived in Honolulu and suddenly found himself responsible for the management of a store.

Almost all of the Chinese migrants were men. Single women did not travel alone to distant places, and married women generally stayed home. Len Mau Nin, for example, did not accompany her 21-year-old husband, Len Wai, a

Not all the Chinese immigrants were farm laborers. Some, like this fish seller in San Francisco's Chinatown, were merchants.

contract laborer who went to Hawaii in 1882. She remained behind in Guangdong because one of her parents was blind and she was needed there. "Also most women didn't want to go to a strange place anyway," her grandson Raymond Len explained, "and leave the so-called comforts of an extended family."

Chinese tradition and culture limited migration for women. A Chinese woman was told to obey her father as a daughter, her husband as a wife, and her eldest son as a widow. A daughter's name was not recorded in the family tree—it was entered later next to her husband's name in *his* family tree. As a daughter-in-law, she was expected to take care of her husband's aging parents. "A boy is born facing in; a girl is born facing out," said a Chinese proverb, revealing the different family roles of sons and daughters.

Women of all classes were regarded as inferior to men. They were expected to stay home, tending to family and domestic duties. The tightly bound feet of upper-class women were a symbol of high social rank. Some Chinese men considered women with bound feet desirable, but these pathetically crippled feet kept women from moving about freely. In 1855 a Chinese merchant of San Francisco explained why many men did not bring their wives with them to America. He said that the women of the "better families" generally had "compressed feet" and were "unused to winds and waves." But it was not only the upper class that kept its women at home. Although peasant women did not have bound feet, they were also tied to family and home and confined within their village walls.

Chinese women were also left behind because it would have cost too much for them to accompany their husbands, and because the men thought they would be gone only temporarily. Another explanation, the "hostage theory," claims that the women were kept at home to make sure that their absent husbands in America would send money home to their families and would return someday. In Chinese peasant culture, each family's household property and land was divided among all adult sons, and the sons shared responsibility for supporting their elderly parents. Parents kept the wives and children of these sons at home, hoping that wandering sons would not forget their families in China. "The mother wanted her son to come back," explained Len Mau Yun. "If wife go to America, then son no go back home and no send money."

Men migrating to Hawaii were more likely to take their wives with them than were men migrating to California.

An upper-class Chinese girl with bound feet. Footbinding, which began in early childhood and was intensely painful, was believed to make women more attractive, but it also kept them from traveling freely.

In 1900, of the 25,767 Chinese in Hawaii, 3,471 or 13.5% were female, but of the 89,863 Chinese on the U.S. mainland, only 4,522 or 5% were female. Why did a much larger percentage of women go to Hawaii than to the continental United States?

Chinese women were more welcome in Hawaii than on the mainland. Hawaii encouraged Chinese women to immigrate. As early as 1864, the editor of the *Pacific Commercial Advertiser* anxiously noted that nearly all of the Chinese on the sugar plantations were men. He recommended that Chinese women should be brought in to keep the men behaving properly: "To throw in these islands, hundreds or thousands of laborers without their wives, to encourage their importation without that controlling and softening influence which women, by God's will, exercise over man, would be to encourage vice and urge on the fearful evils originated by dissolute habits." In 1877, the newspaper editor again worried about so many young Chinese men without wives. "No Chinamen," he insisted in an editorial, "should be allowed henceforth to come here . . . unless they are accompanied by their women."

Missionaries in Hawaii also became alarmed about Chinese male laborers "without women and children" living like "animals" on the plantations. Urging the planters to bring Chinese women to Hawaii, missionary Frank Damon declared, "No surer safeguard can be erected against the thousand possible ills which may arise from the indiscriminate herding together of thousands of men!" Damon believed that "the sweet and gentle influence of the mother, the wife, the sister, and the daughter" would be more effective than the police at keeping the Chinese men in line.

Planters themselves saw that Chinese women could be used to control the Chinese men. In a letter to missionary Damon in 1881, a planter wrote that the presence of Chinese wives and families would reduce the chance of "riotous disturbances" among the Chinese. The planters wanted their workers to be peaceful and productive. If wives would make them peaceful and productive, then they should have wives.

When the Hawaiian Board of Immigration wanted to recruit about 500 Chinese laborers in Hong Kong in 1865, it specified that 20 to 25% of them must be married women. Under this program, Chinese men could afford to take their wives with them to Hawaii, for the planters would pay for the wives' passage. Like the men, the women would sign labor contracts to work on the plantations. Women were to do light

47

labor only, and the planters could not separate them from their husbands. But the women were paid less than the men— $3 rather than $4 a month. Of 528 Chinese laborers recruited under this program, 96 were women; there were also 10 children.

A combination of missionary concern and employer self-interest encouraged the immigration of Chinese women to Hawaii. But these conditions did not exist in California. In fact, California discouraged Chinese women from immigrating. Employers in California viewed Chinese laborers not as settlers but as temporary migrants. The employers wanted a labor force of single men, always ready to move to the next construction site or the next harvest. They did not want to be responsible for families, and they did not care about the social needs of their workers. Their relationship to the workers was businesslike—they were purchasing labor, nothing more.

Chinese men who came to Hawaii saw that their situation would be fairly settled. They would work for five years on a particular plantation where they would live in a stable community. But in California, as miners or railroad workers or migrant farm laborers, Chinese men would be entering a frontier society where living conditions would be difficult for wives and children.

The Chinese were viewed quite differently by whites in California than by whites in Hawaii, and this too explains why fewer Chinese women came to the mainland. In 1879, an

editorial in the Hawaiian missionary paper *The Friend* described the differing white attitudes toward the Chinese: "The California watchword may be 'The Chinese must go,' but that of Hawaii is 'The Chinese must come,' to work our cane and rice fields. Now let us treat them fairly, and do all in our power

to introduce Chinese families and diffuse among them Christianity." Underlying this difference was the presence of a large white working class in California. The white workers viewed Chinese laborers as competitors. In contrast, there were relatively few white workers in Hawaii, so there was less competition and resentment. The Chinese encountered more racial discrimination and hostility, even violence, in California than in Hawaii.

Whites in Hawaii did not see the islands as a place for extensive white settlement. Whites made up only a tiny fraction of Hawaii's population in the late 19th century, so they did not have a mainly white society to preserve or defend. But as early as 1850—only two years after the United States took California from Mexico—whites had begun to turn California into a mostly white society. Seeing the flow of darker faces into California, whites felt the need to protect their way of life. They saw the entry of Chinese women and families as a threat to their view of America as a "white man's country."

Both Hawaii and the United States developed policies to control Chinese immigration, but their policies were very

Two lunas, or overseers, look on while Chinese workers cut sugar cane on the island of Kauai. Rattan hats protected workers against the burning sun; thick clothing was needed to shield them from the sharp leaves.

"The Chinese must come!" said the plantation owners of Hawaii. These workers are planting rice—long the staple crop of south China—in Honolulu.

different. Concerned about the growing presence of a disorderly and overwhelmingly male Chinese population in the 1880s, the Hawaiian government limited Chinese immigration to 2,400 a year. But women and children were not counted in this quota; instead they were encouraged to come.

The policies of the U.S. government, on the other hand, were designed to exclude Chinese women. In 1875 the government passed the Page Law to prevent prostitutes from entering the country. This law was enforced so strictly and broadly, however, that it not only kept out Chinese prostitutes but also discouraged Chinese wives from emigrating. Chinese women seeking to enter the United States had to undergo rigorous questioning by U.S. officials in China, and the prospect of this unpleasant interview was intimidating.

By the 1880s, prejudice against the Chinese was on the rise in the United States. Many white Americans felt that there were already too many Chinese in the country, and they wanted to prevent more from entering. In 1882 Congress passed the Chinese Exclusion Act, a law that prohibited the entry of Chinese laborers for 10 years (it was later extended). At first it was unclear whether this law also restricted the entry of Chinese women. This question was tested two years later in the Circuit Court of California. Too Cheong, a Chinese laborer and resident of the United States, had returned to China in 1883 and married Ah Moy. When he came back to the United States a year later, Too Cheong brought his wife with him. The court refused to let Ah Moy enter the country, declaring that the wife of a Chinese laborer was herself a Chinese laborer and therefore could not lawfully immigrate.

The law was interpreted in such a way as to make almost every Chinese a "laborer," and it was enforced very strictly. In 1888 Congress also said that a Chinese already in the United States could not leave the country and then return. In addition it became unlawful for "any Chinese person" other than a merchant to enter the United States.

Most of the Chinese women who came to Hawaii were wives, but many of those who came to the U.S. mainland in the early years were prostitutes. There were few Chinese prostitutes in Hawaii because Chinese men were allowed to bring their wives to the islands. Chinese immigrants to Hawaii were carefully screened by the government and the planters; this kept out most prostitutes. Furthermore, Chinese men could have relationships with Hawaiian women. Many of them married native women and raised families in the islands.

White Americans' anxieties about Chinese immigration sometimes broke out into violence. Whites in Denver, Colorado, turned against their Chinese neighbors in an 1880 riot.

Unlike their sisters in Hawaii, most of the Chinese women who entered California before 1875 were prostitutes. In 1870, there were 3,536 Chinese women in California, and 2,157 or 61% of them were listed as "prostitutes" in the census. Before the Chinese Exclusion Act, Chinese could enter America voluntarily as immigrants, without the sponsorship of an employer as was necessary in Hawaii. This meant that the United States could not screen out the prostitutes as effectively as Hawaii did. Chinese prostitutes found a place in the United States because the Chinese community in California was largely composed of migratory men. Lacking wives, these men depended on prostitutes to satisfy their sexual needs.

One prostitute, Lilac Chen, was only six years old when she was brought to San Francisco. Years later, at the age of 84, she remembered the day her father said he was taking her to her grandmother's house: "And that worthless father, my own father, imagine . . . sold me on the ferry boat. Locked me in the cabin while he was negotiating my sale." Chen kicked and screamed. When she was finally let out, she could not find her father. "He had left me, you see, with a strange woman."

Another prostitute, Wong Ah So, described her tragic experience: "I was nineteen when this man came to my mother and said that in America there was a great deal of gold. . . . He was a laundryman, but said he earned plenty of money. He was very nice to me, and my mother liked him, so my mother was glad to have me go with him as his wife. I thought that I was his wife, and was very grateful that he was taking me to such a grand, free country, where everyone was rich and

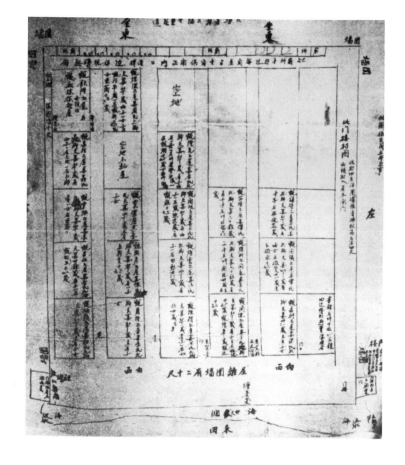

A crib sheet used by an immigrant who hoped to bypass the exclusion laws by posing as a relative of someone already living in the United States. "Paper sons," as these fake relatives were called, faced rigorous questioning at American immigration stations. Their crib sheets were sometimes 200 pages long.

happy." But two weeks after Wong Ah So arrived in San Francisco, she was shocked to learn that her companion had taken her to America as a "slave" and that she would be forced to work as a prostitute.

The Chinese migration to America, however, was mainly the movement of men. They planned to return to China. Waving goodbye, many sojourners heard their wives sing:

Right after we were wed, Husband, you set out on a journey.
How was I to tell you how I felt?
Wandering around a foreign country, when will you ever come
  home?
I beg of you, after you depart, to come back soon,
Our separation will be only a flash of time;
I only wish that you would have good fortune,
In three years you would be home again.
Also, I beg of you that your heart won't change,
That you keep your heart and mind on taking care of your
  family;
Each month or half a month send a letter home,
In two or three years my wish is to welcome you home.

"See you again, see you again," the men shouted. Turning away from their wives, they traveled on foot or in small boats to port cities like Canton and Hong Kong, and there they boarded ships bound for Honolulu and San Francisco.

A Japanese picture bride photographed around 1910. Engaged or even married to a man she had never met, a picture bride entered a new relationship as well as a new culture when she reached America.

Chapter Three

THE JAPANESE CAME LATER THAN THE CHINESE immigrants. They arrived in Hawaii in significant numbers beginning in the 1880s and in the continental United States a decade later. But like the Chinese, the immigrants from Japan—the Issei, or "first generation"—carried a vision of hope. One of them wrote:

> *Huge dreams of fortune*
> *Go with me to foreign lands,*
> *Across the ocean.*

For more than two centuries, the Japanese people had been forbidden by law from traveling to foreign lands. In 1639 Japan began an era of isolation from the West that was not broken until 1853, when Commodore Matthew C. Perry of the United States forced the island kingdom to open its doors. After this intrusion, Japan's rulers continued the ban on emigration, but they found the law hard to enforce. In 1868 the Hawaiian consul general in Japan secretly recruited 148 Japanese contract laborers and took them to Hawaii. A year later a German merchant named John Henry Schnell took some 40 Japanese to California to start a silk farm. In 1884 the Japanese government gave in to the inevitable and let Hawaiian planters recruit contract laborers.

There was an explosion of emigration from Japan. Pressures within the country had been building for a long time. For centuries Japan had been ruled by military leaders called shoguns, who kept real power away from the country's feeble emperors. But in 1868 a group of warlords overthrew

Matthew Perry's American fleet off the coast of Japan in March 1854. Perry forced the Japanese to sign a treaty that would allow U.S. ships to enter Japanese ports.

the shogun and centralized authority under the emperor. Taking the name Meiji, which means "Enlightened Rule," the young emperor established his power in what came to be called the Meiji Restoration.

After the Meiji Restoration, Japan began a fervent program of modernization along Western lines. The country's new leaders believed that the way to protect Japan from European and American powers was to become like them, developing industries and a strong army and navy. To raise money for factories and military equipment, the Meiji government made farmers pay a yearly tax on their land.

At the same time, the government kept the price of rice low, which meant that many farmers could not earn enough from the sale of their crops to pay their taxes. More than 300,000 farmers lost their lands because they could not pay their taxes. The *Japan Weekly Mail* reported in 1884 that "the distress among the agricultural class has reached a point never before attained. Most of the farmers have been unable to pay their taxes, and hundreds of families in one village alone have been compelled to sell their property in order to liquidate their debts."

Farmers all over Japan faced economic hardships. Many moved to Hokkaido, Japan's northernmost island, in search of opportunity. Conditions in the country's southwestern prefectures, or districts, such as Kumamoto, Fukuoka, Hiroshima, and Yamaguchi, were especially terrible. Hiroshima prefecture had less land per household than any other district in Japan. A journalist wrote about Yamaguchi prefecture in 1885: "What strikes me most is the hardships paupers are having in surviving. . . . Their regular fare consists of rice husk or buckwheat chaff ground into powder and the dregs of bean curd mixed with leaves and grass."

Farmers in the stricken southwest were specially recruited as laborers for emigration to Hawaii. During the 1870s, a Hawaiian official named R. W. Irwin had served as adviser to a large Japanese trading company headed by Takashi Masuda. Originally from Yamaguchi, Masuda was concerned about the people suffering there, and he told Irwin to look for laborers in the southwestern prefectures. Once emigration from this area had started, it was urged on by word of mouth as people spoke of the wonderful opportunities in Hawaii.

Thousands of Japan's distressed farmers were seized by an emigration *netsu*—a "fever" to migrate to the Hawaiian

Islands and the United States. They saw themselves as sojourners, laborers working temporarily in a foreign land. Their
goal was to work hard so they could "return home in glory"
after three years and use their savings to buy land—perhaps
the very land they had lost.

Many migrants carried a responsibility to pay family
debts. One of them was the grandfather of Hawaii's Senator
Daniel Inouye. A fire had broken out in the Inouye family
home and spread to nearby houses; to pay for the damages,
the family sent the eldest son, Asakichi, to Hawaii, accompanied by his wife and four-year-old son. He planned to return
to Japan after the family debt had been paid.

The migrants carried in their hearts the dream of
striking it rich and coming back to Japan as *kin'i kikyo*, or
wealthy persons. Some of them hoped to advance into a higher
social class by becoming a *yoshi*—a son-in-law adopted into
the wife's family. "I planned to work three years in the United
States to save 500 yen and then go back to Japan," a migrant
explained, "because if I had 500 yen in Japan I could marry
into a farmer's household, using it for my marriage portion."

Hawaii offered a chance to succeed. During the years
1885–94, when the Japanese government sponsored the emigration of contract laborers, Japanese migrants agreed that if
their passage to Hawaii were paid by the planters, then they
would work for three years for $9 a month plus food, lodging,
and medical care. They clearly saw the advantage they would
have in Hawaii: A plantation laborer in the islands could earn
six times more than a laborer in Japan. The migrants were told
that in three years they would be able to save 400 yen—an
amount that a silk worker in Japan could acquire only by
working every day and saving all wages for 10 years. Three

My uncle, Nobuyoshi Takaki, who immigrated to Hawaii in 1904, and his picture bride, Yukino.

years of separation from family and friends seemed to be a small sacrifice for such a huge sum.

There was no shortage of Japanese eager to make that sacrifice. When the Japanese government announced that it would send 600 emigrants in the first shipment of laborers to Hawaii in 1885, it received 28,000 applications. By 1894, some 30,000 Japanese had gone to the islands as government contract laborers. After 1894, migrants went to the islands as private contract laborers through emigration companies, or as free laborers, using their savings or borrowing money to pay for their passage.

> *Family fortunes*
> *Fall into the wicker trunk*
> *I carry abroad.*

"My father had put a mortgage on his property to get me the 200 yen I used when I sailed to Hawaii," said a migrant. Another one explained, "For the cost to come to Hawaii our land was placed under a mortgage. And we borrowed some money, about $100, from the moneylender. After we came to Hawaii we sent money back. If we didn't pay it back, our land would have been taken away."

Beginning in the 1890s, Japanese migrants were also attracted to the United States mainland. American wages seemed fantastic. They were about $1 a day, or more than 2 yen a day. In 1902, a carpenter in Japan could make only two-thirds of a yen for a day's work. The Japanese migrants thought that "money grew on trees" in America.

Between 1885 and 1924, 200,000 Japanese went to Hawaii and 180,000 went to the mainland. They were mostly young men—my grandfather Kasuke Okawa was only 19 years old when he left home in 1886. Between 40% and 60% of the migrants were in their twenties, and another 25% were in their thirties.

Because Japan's education system required everyone to go to school, the Japanese newcomers were better educated than those from other countries. They had an average of eight years of schooling. In fact, Japanese migrants had a higher literacy rate than Europeans who came to the United States. According to the U.S. census for 1910, only 9.2% of the Japanese immigrants 10 years of age and older were illiterate, compared to 12.7% of the foreign-born whites. Most Japanese migrants came from the farming class and were not desperately poor. The average Japanese man arrived in the United States with more money than his European counterpart.

The Japanese migrants were a select group, more so than the Chinese. Unlike China, Japan was ruled by a strong central government. The Meiji Restoration had unified the country, and the new state was able to control emigration. Driven by a rising nationalism, or sense of national pride and identity, the government viewed Japanese migrants as representatives of their homeland. Anyone who wished to go to Hawaii or the United States had to apply for permission. Review boards screened the applicants to make sure that they were healthy and literate—and would "maintain Japan's national honor" abroad.

The Japanese government did not want the Japanese people to get a bad reputation in America. Japanese officials had seen how Chinese migrants were regarded as inferior in the United States. They had seen laws passed to keep the Chinese out of America, and they believed this was due to the

Emperor Mutsuhito of Japan took the name Meiji, which means "enlightened rule." He ushered in a period of social and economic change that propelled Japan into the modern world.

This picture of my father, Toshio Takaki, was taken in 1918 for his passport. At the age of 13, he taught himself to use a camera and became a professional photographer.

poor quality of the Chinese migrants. In 1884 Japanese consul Shinkichi Takahashi reported: "It is indeed the ignominious conduct and behavior of indigent Chinese of inferior character . . . that brought upon the Chinese as a whole the contempt of the Westerners and resulted in the enactment of legislation to exclude them from the country." He warned against letting poor and ignorant migrants go the United States, or else the Japanese would soon follow "in the wake of the Chinese."

Seven years later, as Japanese migrants began entering the United States, Japanese consul Sutemi Chinda similarly warned that if the government permitted the emigration of "lower class Japanese," it would give the Americans an excuse to ban all Japanese from their country. The Chinese "failure" in America, Chinda stressed, must be a "lesson" for Japan.

Japanese women went to America in much larger numbers than Chinese women. Fearing that a mostly male population would encounter problems with prostitution, gambling, and drunkenness, the Japanese government encouraged women to emigrate along with men. As early as 1905, women made up more than 22% of the Japanese population in Hawaii and about 7% on the mainland. Three years later, in a treaty with the United States called the Gentlemen's Agreement, Japan agreed to limit the emigration of Japanese "laborers." But there was a loophole: Parents, wives, and children of laborers already in America would be allowed to emigrate. This policy allowed my uncle Nobuyoshi Takaki, who came to Hawaii in 1904, to send for his father Santaro in 1912. Santaro, in turn, was joined by his two remaining sons, Teizo and Toshio, in 1918. Toshio, who would become my father, was 13 years old when he arrived.

Thousands of women entered Hawaii and the mainland through that loophole—66,926 of them between 1908 and 1924. Between 1911 and 1920, women represented 39% of all Japanese entering the islands or the mainland. By 1920 women accounted for 46% of all Japanese in Hawaii and 35% of all Japanese on the mainland. A year later Japan and the United States negotiated the Ladies' Agreement, in which Japan agreed to stop sending picture brides abroad. But by then some 20,000 picture brides, including my aunts Yukino Takaki and Mitsue Takaki, had already arrived in the United States.

The picture bride system, or "photo-marriage," was based on the Japanese custom of arranged marriage. Marriage

65

The Japanese migration to Hawaii included many women The wives of farmers toiled for long hours in the fields and orchards and also shouldered the burdens of housework and caring for the children.

in Japanese society was not an individual matter but rather a family concern. Parents used go-betweens to help them select partners for their sons and daughters. When families lived far apart, the bride and groom often exchanged photographs before their first meeting. This traditional practice lent itself readily to the needs of Japanese migrants in America.

Picture bride Ai Miyasakai later recalled, "When I told my parents about my desire to go to a foreign land, the story spread throughout the town. From here and there requests for marriage came pouring in just like rain!" Riyo Orite, who came to the United States in 1913, also had a "picture marriage." Her marriage to a Japanese man in America had been arranged through a relative. "All agreed to our marriage," she said, "but I didn't get married immediately. I was engaged at the age of sixteen and didn't meet Orite until I was almost eighteen. I had seen him only in a picture at first."

Another reason Japanese women emigrated more freely than Chinese women was that women's lives in Japan were changing. Although women in China were restricted to the farm and the home, women in 19th-century Japan were becoming wage-earning workers. Thousands of young women worked away from home in inns and bars as well as in such industries as tea processing and papermaking. During the 1880s, daughters of farming families made up 80% of textile workers. Women were often hired as construction laborers, and they also worked in the coal mines, where they carried heavy loads of coal on their backs out of the tunnels.

By 1900, 60% of Japan's industrial laborers were women. Women in rural areas were leaving home for work almost as commonly as men. This pattern became more widespread as the Meiji government promoted modernization and industrialization in order to create a strong and prosperous nation that could protect itself from Western powers. The migration of Japanese women to Hawaii and the United States was just the next step in a movement of women that was already well underway in Japan.

Japanese women also liked the idea of traveling overseas more than Chinese women did. The Meiji government required education for girls, declaring in 1872 that "girls should be educated . . . alongside boys." Emperor Meiji himself promoted female education. "My country is now undergoing a complete change from old to new ideas, which I completely desire," he said. Japanese youth, "boys as well as girls," should learn about foreign countries and become "enlightened as to ideas of the world."

Japanese women were more likely than their Chinese counterparts to be able to read and write. "I attended six years of elementary school: two years of Koto sho gakko [middle advanced elementary school], and four years of girls' middle school," said Michiko Tanaka. "We studied English and Japanese, mathematics, literature, writing, and religion." In 1876 the Japanese school system was redesigned, and English was adopted as a major subject in middle school.

Girls and women in Japan were curious about the outside world. They had been told by Emperor Meiji how women "should be allowed to go abroad" and how Japan would "benefit by the knowledge thus acquired." They also heard stories describing America as "heavenly," and many of them were more eager to see the new land than to meet their new husbands there.

"I wanted to see foreign countries and besides I had consented to marriage with Papa because I had the dream of seeing America," Michiko Tanaka revealed to her daughter years later. "I wanted to see America and Papa was a way to get there." Another picture bride said, "I was bubbling over with great expectations. My young heart, 19 years and 8 months old, burned, not so much with the prospects of reuniting with my new husband, but with the thought of the New World." Told that they would be married and sent to husbands in America, many women secretly had their own reasons for going—reasons such as curiosity, ambition, and a sense of adventure.

The emigration of women was also influenced by Japanese tradition. A folk saying popular among Japanese farmers expressed traditional views about the roles of their children: "One to sell, one to follow, and one in reserve." The "one to sell" was the daughter, who was expected to marry and join her husband's family. "Once you become someone's wife you belong to his family," explained Tsuru Yamaguchi. She found out she would be going to Hawaii somewhat

O. TAKAYAMA'S SEED RICE FARM
SUNSET ROUTE
OCEAN TO OCEAN

Japanese farmers made important contributions to American agriculture, first in California and then in other states. These men worked on a Japanese-owned farm in Deepwater, Texas, that sold rice seeds to other farmers.

abruptly: "I learned about the marriage proposal when we had to exchange pictures." Emigration for her was not a choice but rather an obligation as a wife.

Whether a Japanese woman went to America depended on which son she married—the son "to follow" or the son "in reserve." Unlike the Chinese, who divided their land among all of their sons, Japanese farmers passed their land on to only one son, usually the oldest. The land could not be broken up into smaller parcels: This custom kept farms intact in this mountainous island nation, where farmland was limited. Most of the farm holdings were small. Breaking them up into still smaller holdings would have created plots too tiny to support a family.

As the possessor of the family farm, the oldest son, the "one to follow," was responsible for taking care of the parents when they became old. The younger boys, the sons "in reserve," had to find work in towns. They were used to leaving home to find jobs in Japan, and this pattern could be easily applied to looking for jobs abroad. At the morning ceremonies of the elementary and middle schools, principals told their students, "First sons, stay in Japan and be men of Japan. Second sons, go abroad with great ambition as men of the world!" The Japanese younger sons who became laborers in foreign lands were not as tightly bound to their parents as Chinese sons were. They were allowed to take their wives and children with them to distant lands.

But some first sons also emigrated—my uncle Nobuyoshi Takaki was the oldest son in his family. Many first sons came when they were young, before their parents grew elderly and dependent. Others came to earn money to add to

Japanese businessmen called labor contractors ran employment agencies that found work for the migrants. The contractor would take a percentage of each worker's earnings as his commission.

70

the family incomes and help pay family debts. First sons sometimes took their wives with them, thinking that with two incomes they could pay off family debts more quickly and shorten their sojourn abroad. Younger sons were even more likely to take their wives, for they could stay away longer—perhaps forever.

The migration of Japanese women also depended on the policies and conditions of the receiving countries. For example, the United States government had strictly prohibited the entry of Chinese women, but it allowed Japanese women to come under the Gentlemen's Agreement.

Because the Japanese came to the United States later than the Chinese, they entered a more stable and developed society. Although most Chinese laborers had moved from place to place to work in mines or on railroads, thousands of Japanese immigrant men settled down to become shopkeepers and small farmers. They sent for their wives, who could assist them as unpaid family labor. Wives were particularly useful on farms that required a lot of labor. "Nearly all of these tenant farmers are married and have their families with them," one observer noted in a report on the Japanese in California in 1915. "The wives do much work in the fields."

The U.S. government allowed the entry of Japanese women, but the Hawaiian government actually encouraged it. In 1879, Hawaii insisted that 40% of the immigrants should be women. Half the cost of their passage would be paid by the Hawaiian Bureau of Immigration, and they would receive $6 a month in wages, compared to $10 for men. Between 1885 and 1894, the Bureau of Immigration systematically recruited Japanese women, who made up 20% of contract laborers sponsored by the Japanese government. And between 1894 and 1908, thousands of women sailed to Hawaii as private laborers. One of them was my grandmother Katsu Okawa, who emigrated as a single woman in 1896.

Unlike the farmers on the United States mainland who wanted a male work force, the Hawaiian planters viewed Japanese women as workers: cooks, seamstresses, and field laborers. Planters also saw that they could use families to control the men. In 1886, a year after the Japanese movement to the islands began, an immigration official in Hawaii reported that Japanese men who had their wives with them worked better and were more satisfied with their situations. "Several of the planters," he noted, "are desirous that each man [from Japan] should have his wife."

After 1900, when Hawaii became a territory of the United States, planters became even more anxious to bring Japanese women. Federal law now prohibited the contract labor system; so the planters had to make their laborers want to stay on the plantations. Realizing that men with wives were more likely to stay than single men, planters asked their business agents in Honolulu to send "men with families." The manager of the Hutchinson Sugar Plantation, for example, wrote to a labor supply company in 1905: "Will you be kind enough to send us as soon as you are able to do so, forty Japanese married couples. We want them for the Hilea section of the Plantation where we have always had more or less trouble in keeping Japanese laborers, and believe that by having married couples only, the laborers would remain."

Many women were brought from Japan as prostitutes. Most of them went to the United States mainland. Some were sold to Japanese pimps; others were kidnapped or lured under false pretenses. The daughter of a farming family later recounted her experience. In 1890, a "smooth-talking" salesman told her stories about foreign lands. He said that "gold nuggets were waiting to be picked up on the riverbanks of America," and he persuaded her to accompany him to nearby Nagasaki, where he showed her a foreign ship bound for America. After boarding the huge ship, she walked the decks enjoying the new experience. Then she was introduced to a sailor, who said, "Why don't you go to America on the ship?" "I'd like to go and see America," she replied, "but since I don't know anyone there, I can't." Just as she was "half thinking about wanting to go and half worrying," she heard a bell clang. The ship hoisted anchor and sailed out of port. The salesman was nowhere to be seen. The sailor took her to a cabin and warned her, "I'll bring you meals; so don't leave the room. If by chance you're discovered, you'll be thrown into the sea." When the ship reached San Francisco, the sailor dressed her in Western clothes and took her off the ship. "Pulled by his hand in the pitch darkness of the night," she followed him to a house where she was forced to become a prostitute.

Most Japanese migrants, however, left home voluntarily, looking forward to their adventure. Yet as they prepared to leave their farms and villages, they felt the anxiety of separation. One of them remembered how her brother-in-law had said farewell: "Don't stay in the [United] States too long. Come back in five years and farm with us." But her father then said, "Are you kidding? They can't learn anything in five years. They'll even have a baby over there. . . . Be patient for twenty years." Her father's words shocked her so much she began to cry. Suddenly she realized how long the separation could be.

73

With tears in my eyes
I turn back to my homeland,
Taking one last look.

"My parents came to see me off at Kobe station," a woman recalled many years later. "They did not join the crowd, but quietly stood in front of the wall. They didn't say 'good luck,' or 'take care,' or anything. They did not say one word of encouragement to me. They couldn't say anything because they knew, as I did, that I would never return."

Many migrants wondered if they would ever see Japan again. Perhaps they were destined to live and die abroad, "to become the soil of the foreign land." Realizing that her stay in America would be a permanent one, a woman expressed her feelings in poetry:

Parting tearfully,
Holding a one-way ticket
I sailed for America.

There were settlers as well as sojourners among the migrants. "My father came here as a non-sojourner," said Frank S. Miyamoto of Seattle. "He had the idea that he would stay." His father had gone to Korea first and then crossed to the United States to become a merchant. He had little reason to return to Japan, for he was an only son and both of his parents had died.

Frank Tomori of Portland, Oregon, also saw America as his new home. He recalled, "I happened to see a Western movie, called 'Rodeo,' at the Golden Horse Theater in Okayama City, and was completely obsessed with 'American fever' as a result of watching cowboys dealing with tens of thousands of horses in the vast Western plains. Enormous continent! Rich land! One could see a thousand miles at a glance! Respect for freedom and equality! That must be my permanent home, I decided."

After 1908 Japanese immigration shifted from sojourning to settling. The new slogan of Japanese immigrants was "stay in America and make it your country." More and more of them saw that their stay in the United States would be a long one, or even a permanent one. They summoned their families to join them.

As they left their homes, the migrants drew inspiration and strength from their legends. One story was about Momotaro, the peach-boy. An old childless couple lived on a farm. One day the woman went down to the stream to wash clothes and saw a large peach floating in the water. She brought the fruit home, and her husband cut it open. They were surprised to find a baby boy in the peach. Momotaro grew up to be a strong and brave warrior—an expert swordsman, a samurai for the people—and he went off to fight the demons who were threatening the village. After destroying the monsters, Momotaro returned home and took care of his parents for the rest of their lives. As they gathered their courage within them for the long journey that lay ahead, most of the migrants promised that they, too, would return. Homesickness mingled with excitement. One of them wrote:

> *Mine a Meiji voice,*
> *Crossing the Pacific sea,*
> *It has grown husky.*

The Koreans were the third group of Asians to migrate to America. They left their homeland not just to seek new opportunities but also to escape political repression and unrest.

Chapter Four

Leaving the Land of Morning Calm

THE NEXT GROUP OF ASIANS TO EMIGRATE TO AMERICA came from Korea. Between 1903 and 1920, about 8,000 Koreans left their homeland, which they called the kingdom of Choson ("Morning Calm"). Most of them went to Hawaii, but some went to the U.S. mainland.

Like the Chinese and Japanese, the Korean migrants were young. More than 90% of the adults were between the ages of 16 and 44. But the Koreans differed from the Chinese and Japanese. Although many of the Chinese and Japanese migrants came from farming communities, most of the Koreans came from the cities. They were urban laborers, government clerks, students, policemen, miners, domestic servants, and even Buddhist monks. Their level of education was closer to that of the Japanese than that of the Chinese—about 70% of them could read and write.

About 40% of all Korean immigrants were Christians. They had been converted and encouraged to emigrate by American missionaries. "I was born in Korea," said one migrant, "and was a Christian before I came to the United States." At large tent meetings in the Korean seaport of Inchon, Reverend George Heber Jones of the Methodist Episcopal Church preached to the would-be emigrants and filled them with high ambitions. According to Tae-song Yi of the Korean Christian Movement of Hawaii, American missionaries appeared in Korea and began telling them about "the wonderful story of the Cross." The new converts were told that Hawaii was a "haven of peace and plenty."

The Korean migration was also driven by political events. Japan invaded Korea in 1904, and six years later Japan formally claimed ownership of Korea. After this annexation, Koreans went to Hawaii to escape from Japanese imperialism. "There was little or no opportunity for my grandfather to find a job in Korea in those days," a Korean in Hawaii explained. "The Japanese imperial government was controlling Korea at the time and the outlook toward the future was very poor." The Japanese were "cruel oppressors," he added. "When my grandfather learned that the Japanese government was letting people out of the country to work in the islands, he was happy to volunteer."

Hawaii was also a place where Koreans could struggle for their homeland's independence. "When I saw my country fall into the hands of the Japanese aggressors," said a migrant, "I was filled with sorrow, but, unable to do much to help, I applied for the status of an immigrant and came to Hawaii hoping to learn something in order to help my country."

Some Korean migrants left as political refugees, escaping from Japanese persecution. Sa-sun Whang, a high-school teacher in Korea during the early years of the Japanese occupation, joined a secret Korean patriotic society. "At the time the Japanese military government persecuted the people, especially the young people, and took them to jail," said Whang. To avoid being arrested by the Japanese police for belonging to the society, he left Korea. "My wife and I sneaked out. . . ," he recalled. "We crossed the Yalu River and from there rode the railroad to Shanghai. At that time I wore Chinese clothes. The Japanese didn't know I was Korean; they

thought I was Chinese." In Shanghai, Whang and his wife boarded a ship bound for America. "When I left Korea, I felt like a free man. Korea was like a jail, and I was a prisoner. I wanted to come to America. America was a free country."

Myung-ja Sur also left Korea for political reasons. "Because the Japanese oppression was so severe for all

Japanese troops wearing Western-style uniforms launch an attack across a bridge in Korea. After Japan invaded Korea in 1904, many Korean patriots fled the country.

Koreans, especially Korean patriots, I had to flee to Shanghai," she told her grandson years later. She had been a schoolteacher and had taken part in a Korean nationalist demonstration in 1919, passing out copies of the Declaration of Independence

A Korean sugar worker on a Hawaiian plantation. Most Korean migrants went to Hawaii, although some went to the American mainland.

and Korean flags. "The Japanese went crazy. They beat up people and killed thousands of Koreans while many were arrested and later killed." In Shanghai, Sur was arrested by the Japanese secret police and imprisoned for a month. "When I returned to Korea the Japanese followed me everywhere so I decided to leave for America where I planned to continue my education. Before I left I sent my picture to this Korean man in the United States and he sent me his picture and then we were married."

But, like the Chinese and Japanese, Korean migrants were also pushed from their homes by poverty. Famine and drought had brought suffering to Korea. One American missionary described the terrible conditions: "We have never known such unrest among the Koreans due to the excitement of so many going to the Hawaiian Islands to work on sugar plantations, and the dreadful hardtimes. . . . We can't blame them for wanting to go to America."

In a letter to Governor Sanford Dole of Hawaii in 1902, an American official in Korea reported: "The severe famine of the past winter made the matter [of emigrating to Hawaii] seem all the more attractive to the people." The following year, on January 27, a leader of the sugar industry in Hawaii described the arrival of the first group of Korean immigrants: "We have just received about fifty laborers and their families from Korea. As the people there are in a starving condition we hope that we shall be able to get a number of them as they seem to be just what our plantations need."

"Times were hard," a Korean immigrant recalled. "The country had been passing through a period of famine years. . . . My occupation as tax collector barely kept me from

Korean students of a church-sponsored school in Honolulu. Many Korean immigrants were Christians, and their churches played a vital role in their communities, providing social as well as religious services.

starvation's door as I travelled from village to village." At first he planned to migrate alone and return to Korea after three years, but he finally decided to take his family with him to America.

Another Korean recalled, "We left Korea because we were too poor." Crying at the memory of the suffering, she added, "We had nothing to eat. There was absolutely no way we could survive."

Echoing her story, another migrant said, "There were no opportunities for work of any kind and conditions were bad. It was then that we heard of a man who was talking a lot about the opportunities in Hawaii. He said it was a land of opportunity where everybody was rich."

From newspaper advertisements and posters, Koreans learned that plantation laborers in Hawaii received free housing, medical care, and $16 a month in exchange for working 60 hours each week. These wages equaled about 64 *won* (Korean dollars)—a small fortune to Koreans. Emigrants were told by the labor recruiters that Hawaii was a "paradise" where "clothing grew on trees, free to be picked," and where "gold dollars were blossoming on every bush." America was described as a "land of gold" and a "land of dreams." Lured by fantasy and hope, Koreans borrowed money from a bank that was financed by the Hawaiian sugar planters. The emigrants agreed that the $100 loan for their passage to Hawaii would be deducted by the plantation manager from their monthly pay over a three-year period.

The Korean migration included many women. Of the 6,685 adults who entered Hawaii or the U.S. mainland between 1903 and 1906, nearly 10% were women. Because they were guaranteed jobs and housing on the plantations, Korean men saw the islands as a place where family life was possible. But many took their wives and children with them because they were afraid that they would not be able to return to a Korea that was dominated by the Japanese.

Another 1,066 Korean women came as picture brides between 1906 and 1923. Japanese picture-marriages were arranged by families, but Korean migrants had to rely on Japanese agents to make the arrangements for them. In their offices in the port cities, agents displayed photographs of grooms and gathered applications from interested young Korean women. At the time of their marriages, the men were generally 20 years older than their wives. By 1920, more than one-fifth of all adult Korean immigrants in the United States were women.

For many Korean picture brides, America promised a better life. "My parents were very poor," said a Korean woman. "One year, a heavy rain came, a flood; the crops all washed down. Oh, it was a very hard time. . . . Under the Japanese, no freedom. Not even free talking." She had heard stories about the islands: "Hawaii's a free place, everybody living well. Hawaii had freedom, so if you like talk, you can talk; you like work, you can work. I wanted to come, so, I sent my picture. Ah, marriage! Then I could get to America! That land of freedom with streets paved of gold! Since I became ten, I've been forbidden to step outside our gates, just like the rest of the girls of my days. So becoming a picture bride would be my answer and release."

Anxious to seek greater opportunity and freedom in America, many more Korean men and women would have left the Land of Morning Calm if the period of emigration had lasted longer. In 1905, only two years after the arrival of the first Korean plantation laborers in Hawaii, Japan began to tighten its hold on Korea. The Japanese government outlawed Korean emigration so that the Koreans could not compete with Japanese laborers for jobs in Hawaii, and also to cut off the flow of migrants who might support Korean independence activities in the United States. As a result of this ban on emigration, Koreans came to America in much smaller numbers than the Chinese and Japanese.

Yet, like the other Asian migrants, Koreans carried with them a sense of expectation. As they crossed the Pacific Ocean to Hawaii, they said to themselves: *Kaeguk chinch wi*— "the country is open, go forward."

Farm workers from the Philippines. Unlike other Asian immigrants, the Filipinos came from a U.S. territory. The great majority of them were young, single men hoping to return to the Philippines with enough money to live well there.

Chapter Five

Manongs
in Movement

UNLIKE THE CHINESE, JAPANESE, AND KOREANS, THE Filipino migrants came from a territory of the United States. The Philippines had been a Spanish colony for centuries, but the United States annexed the islands in 1898, after defeating Spain in the Spanish-American War; that same year the United States also annexed Hawaii. These annexations opened the door for people from the Philippines to enter both Hawaii and the U.S. mainland. The Filipinos who came to America in the first wave of immigration were called by the affectionate term *manongs*.

Filipinos migrated by the tens of thousands—first to Hawaii in the early 1900s and then to the mainland in the 1920s. They had been in contact with European culture for a long time through the Catholic Church, which took root in the Philippines during centuries of Spanish colonial rule: 90% of the migrants were Catholic. "The Filipinos were brought up under Christianity for 400 years," explained immigrant Phillip V. Vera Cruz, pointing out how Filipinos differed from other Asian migrants. "They have a different upbringing and were more attached to the western people."

The Filipinos were also American in their outlook. Many had been educated in schools founded by Americans. "From the time of kindergarten on our islands," said Salvadore del Fierro, "we stood in our short pants and saluted the Stars and Stripes which waved over our schoolyards." In their classrooms they looked at pictures of Washington and Lincoln, studied the Declaration of Independence, and read English-language textbooks about the "home of the free and the brave."

87

"We said the 'Pledge of Allegiance' to the American flag each morning," recalled Angeles Amoroso, who emigrated to the United States in 1923. "We also sang 'The Star Spangled Banner.' All of the classes were taught in English." Thousands of American teachers had gone to the Philippine Islands to Americanize the Filipinos. "I studied under American teachers, learning American history and English, being inspired by those teachers and American ideals," a Filipino told an interviewer in California in 1930. "It's no wonder that I have always wanted to come here."

By 1930, some 110,000 Filipinos had gone to Hawaii and another 40,000 to the mainland. Some of them were students. But the vast majority were laborers from poor and uneducated farming families. The Filipino migration was overwhelmingly composed of young men. Of the 31,092 Filipinos who entered California between 1920 and 1929, 84% were under 30 years of age. Genevieve Laigo of Seattle never forgot how the Filipino men greatly outnumbered the women on the ship carrying them to America in 1929—there were 300 men and only 2 women!

In 1930, only 10,486 or 17% of the 63,052 Filipinos in Hawaii were women. The imbalance between Filipino men and women was even greater on the U.S. mainland. Only 2,941 or 7% of the 45,208 Filipinos on the mainland were women.

More Filipino women went to Hawaii than to the mainland because different labor conditions awaited them at each destination. Filipino laborers were more likely to take their wives to Hawaii, where they would live and work in a permanent, stable plantation community. On the mainland,

Filipino men would be migratory farm laborers, moving from field to field, from one temporary camp to another, even from one state to another—not the sort of life most men wanted for their wives.

In addition, planters in Hawaii knew that it was in their interest to encourage Filipino women to come to the islands. The planters found that men with families were steadier workers than single men: Japanese men, many of whom were married, worked more days a month than Filipino men, most of whom were single. To encourage Filipino men to have families on the plantation and thus become better workers, the planters decided to import Filipino women. An official in the sugar industry wrote: "If these men will furnish us with letters to their wives or prospective wives, photographs of themselves and letters from the managers and from some Filipino women in the camps recommending the men as being desirable husbands, we will endeavor to induce the wives or prospective wives to come to Hawaii, and will see that they reach the men who send for them."

But Filipino culture, with its Spanish and Catholic traditions, prevented women from leaving the Philippines in large numbers. Custom limited the possibilities of travel for women, who had to be accompanied by their husbands or fathers. Also Filipino migrants generally viewed themselves as sojourners, not settlers. They did not see the United States, especially the mainland, as a place to bring families and to settle.

Most of the Chinese and Japanese migrants were married; they either left their wives at home or brought them along. Most of the migrating Filipino men, however, were single. Only 18% of them were married, and most of these left their wives in the Philippines, thinking their stay in the United States would be only temporary.

Thousands of these Filipino men had been forced to leave home. In the Philippines, many migrants said, they found themselves "sinking down into the toilet." Life was getting harder, and people had to "reach farther and farther away to make ends meet." Times had not always been so terrible. In a poem about his early childhood in the Philippines, an immigrant in California depicted a moment of happiness and plenty:

> *My father was a working man*
> *In the land of the big rains,*
> *The water glistened on his arms*
> *Like the cool dew in the morning*
> *When the rice was growing tall. . . .*

"In the forest behind us," a plantation laborer in Hawaii recalled as he talked about his childhood in the Philippines, "we got so much to live on. I would go hunting there with a string trap once a month and you would have to call me clumsy if I brought down less than four wild chickens. We used to trap wild pigs there too and deer." But then "the rich people" from town came with guns to hunt, killing all the game for sport.

As time went on, peasants in the Philippines discovered that their fertile rice lands were being bought up by men who never saw their property, by "names on pieces of paper." Each year the farmers had to give a larger share of their crops to distant landlords. Many farmers were driven into debt. A

Filipinos from poor, uneducated farming families were forced to leave their homes by high taxes and by the loss of their land to moneylenders or wealthy landowners from the cities.

Filipino immigrant remembered his father saying to his brother Luciano:

> "The moneylender has taken my land, son."
>
> "How much more do you owe him, Father?" asked Luciano.
>
> "It is one hundred pesos," said my father. "I promised to pay in three weeks, but he won't listen to me. I'd thought that by that time the rice would be harvested and I could sell some of it; then I would be able to pay him. He sent two policemen to Mangusmana to see that I do not touch the rice. It is my own rice and land. Is it possible, son? Can a stranger take away what we have molded with our hands?"
>
> "Yes, Father," said Luciano. "It is possible under the present government."

Many years after he had left the Philippines, another Filipino immigrant sadly described this process of dispossession. "There was a time when my ancestors owned almost the whole town of Bulac and the surrounding villages. But when the Americans came conditions changed. Little by little my father's lands were sold. My share was mortgaged finally to keep the family from starvation and I soon found myself tilling the soil as did the poor Filipino peasants."

The farmers experienced not only hardships but also personal abuse from the wealthier Filipinos. A young boy never forgot one such incident. One day he went with his mother into town to sell beans. There they saw an elegantly dressed young woman walking down the street. Angered by their stares, the wealthy woman contemptuously struck their basket with her umbrella, scattering the beans on the pavement. Crawling on her knees, the boy's mother scooped the beans into the basket. "It is all right. It is all right," she tried to reassure her son. Confused and stunned, the boy knew it was not all right. He knelt on the wet cement and picked the dirt and pebbles from the beans.

But there was a way out of poverty, Filipinos believed. They could go to America—Hawaii and California. "*Kasla glorya ti Hawaii*," they said: "Hawaii is like a land of glory." They would find work on the sugar plantations and "pick up" money. Then they would return home in triumph and success. Like peacocks, they would strut down the dusty streets of their villages, proudly showing off their "Amerikana" suits, silk shirts, sport shoes, and Stetson hats. They fancied themselves looking so rich with "money to blow."

"Everyone," reported a Filipino immigrant, "became fascinated by the tales told of Hawaii," seized by what was commonly known as the "Hawaiian fever." Labor agents

A Filipino named Nicholas sent home this picture of himself at the wheel of a car. Such pictures filled other young men with "Hawaiian fever."

called "drummers" were sent by the Hawaiian sugar planters to the Philippines to spread this fever. They traveled from town to town, showing movies of the "glorious adventure and the beautiful opportunities" awaiting Filipino workers in Hawaii. These movies were free and were usually shown in the town square so that everybody could see them. A typical scene from one such movie showed workers receiving checks.

The labor agents "dazzled the Filipino eyes" with the sum of $2 a day, a very good wage compared with the 15 cents a man could earn daily by hard labor in the Philippines. "The migrating Filipino," reported the *Manila Times*, "sees no opportunity for him in the Philippines." Lured to the United States in the 1920s, Ted Tomol told an interviewer many years later when he was 83 years old, "Back home, we thought California was the Eldorado"—the legendary land of gold.

Trying to climb out of debt and servitude, Filipinos signed labor contracts. They agreed to work for three years in exchange for transportation to Hawaii and wages of $18 a month plus housing, water, fuel, and medical care. Decades later, a Filipino vividly remembered the day he signed his labor contract:

> The agent was just coming down the steps when I halted my horse in front of the recruiter's office. He was a fellow Filipino, but a Hawaiian.
> "Where are you going?" he asked.
> "I would like to present myself for Hawaii, Apo," I answered as I came down from my horse.
> "Wait, I'll go see if I can place you on the next load," he said, and turned back up into the door.
> When he came out, he had a paper in his hand.

"Come up, so we can fill in the forms," he waved; so
I went in.

"You write?" he asked.

"No," I said; so he filled in for me.

"Come back Monday for the doctor to check you up,"
he said, patting me on the back. "When you come

"Hawaii is a land of glory,"
they said back in the Philippines.
But those who went to the sugar
plantations found that the work
was hot, hard, and exhausting.

back, bring *beinte cinco*, twenty-five, and I'll make sure of your papers for a place," he said, shaking my hand. It was like that. "Tip" is what we call it here. But that is our custom to *pasoksok*, slipsome, for a favor.

The migrants promised to be gone for only three years, for they believed it would be easy to save money in America. Returning with rolls of cash bulging in their pockets, they would pay off the mortgages on their lands and recover their family homes. "My sole ambition was to save enough

Three young Filipina women. Because of religion and customs, single women from the Philippines were not encouraged to emigrate. Those that did found themselves in great demand by Filipino men.

money to pay back the mortgage on my land," explained a Filipino. "In the Philippines a man is considered independent and is looked upon with respect by his neighbors if he possesses land." As he said farewell to his brother in the Philippines, one Filipino laborer promised, "I will come back and buy that house. I will buy it and build a high cement wall around it. I will come back with lots of money and put on a new roof. . . . Wait and see!"

But not all of the departing Filipinos were sojourners. Some knew that they would not be coming back. Rufina Clemente Jenkins had met an American soldier in the Philippines during the Spanish-American War and married him in 1900 when she was only 14 years old. Two years later she sailed to America with her daughter Francesca to join her husband and make her home with him. Pete Silifan of Seattle said that he had come to the United States "to look for a better living. Down there [in the Philippines] we didn't have any future."

Aware that the Philippines offered limited opportunities for education and jobs, especially for women, Angeles Amoroso decided to search for a new future in the United States. "My father had the impression I would be away only for seven years," she said later, "but I knew in my heart that I would be making America my permanent home."

Sikh immigrants from India leave their ship at Vancouver, Canada's western port. Many emigrants from India went to Canada because both nations were part of the British Empire.

Chapter Six

From the Plains of the Punjab

IN 1907, A YEAR AFTER THE FIRST GROUP OF FILIPINOS had landed in Hawaii, workers from India began arriving on the West Coast. The period of Asian-Indian immigration was extremely short. In 1909 U.S. immigration officials began limiting immigration from India, and eight years later Congress banned it completely. Altogether, only 6,400 Asian Indians came to America. The Asian Indians included a smaller percentage of women than any of the other groups of Asian immigrants. Less than 1% were women. Most were young men, from 16 to 35 years of age; many, perhaps most, were married. In 1907, a researcher who interviewed many of the Asian-Indian migrants reported that "practically all" of the newcomers were married and had families in India.

The migrants possessed little or no education; 47% were illiterate. Most had been unskilled laborers and agricultural workers in India. They came to America in small groups of cousins and village neighbors. They had left the fertile plains of the Punjab, the "land of five rivers," a province in northern India that is now divided between India and Pakistan. Most of the migrants were Sikhs, followers of a religion called Sikhism, which blended elements of Islam and Hinduism. To demonstrate their religious commitment, the men never shaved their beards or cut their hair. They wore turbans, for their faith required them to cover their heads in the temple. Many of them shared the name Singh ("lion"), a sacred name to Sikhs.

Of all the immigrants in America, said immigrant Saint N. Singh in 1909, none surpassed the Sikhs in "picturesqueness." They could be seen "clad in countless curious styles." Yards upon yards of cotton or silk were swathed about their heads in turbans, cone-shaped or round like a button mushroom, with waves or points directly in the middle of their foreheads or to the right or left, "as variable as the styles of American women's pompadours."

Asian Indians left their homeland partly because the British had been ruling India since the middle of the 18th century. The British government wanted to run India's agriculture on Western lines, with large farms and plantations instead of small family holdings. Traditional rules of land ownership were changed, and small landholders found themselves in trouble. To pay their debts, many of them had to mortgage their land. Greedy and crooked moneylenders made the peasant farmers sign mortgage contracts that charged high interest rates. If the farmers could not make their payments, they were forced to sell their land.

To make matters worse, famine raged from 1899 to 1902, killing cattle and plunging the peasants deeper into debt. Hoping to escape poverty and misery, Indians by the hundreds of thousands left their homeland to work in British-held territory in the West Indies, Uganda (in Africa), Mauritius (an island in the Indian Ocean), and Guyana (in South America). And several thousand went to Canada and the United States. "Do you wonder when you look at India, with its low wages and high taxes, its famines and plagues, its absence of all incentive toward advancement, that the dam which for so long has held the people in check is weakening?" observed a writer in the *Pacific Monthly Magazine* in 1907. "Do you wonder that the East Indians are turning their faces westward toward the land of progress and opportunity?"

Many Sikhs first left home by enlisting in the British army.
This private in the 16th Bengal Lancers fought in the Boxer
Rebellion in China.

Many Asian Indians chose Canada as their destination because both Canada and India were part of the British Empire. They arrived in Vancouver, the capital of British Columbia, but they found themselves unwelcome there. It seemed that the Canadians were friendly toward the Indians— but not on Canadian soil. "British Columbians are proud of India . . . proud of East Indians as boys of the flag," declared the *Vancouver World* in 1906. "But an East Indian in Canada is out of place." White Canadian workers also complained about the entry of Asian Indians, saying, "British Columbia is a white man's country. The coming hordes of Asiatic laborers will keep wages down and crowd the white man to the wall, since a white man cannot nor will not come down to the Asiatic laborer's low standard of living."

A letter written in 1914 on behalf of 600 Sikhs in Hong Kong, addressed to their friends in America, expressed their fear of a Canadian immigration law that would keep them out of Canada. The letter said, "For God's sake, help us get to the United States or Canada. The new Canadian law will go into effect on 5 March 1914 after which time few Hindus will be admitted into Canada. It has been much more difficult for the past six months to get into Manila than heretofore. We are shut out of Australia and New Zealand. For God's sake, come to our assistance so that we will be able to get into the United States or Canada."

The Indian migrants were sojourners, not settlers. When asked why he had left the Punjab, Deal Singh Madhas told an interviewer, "To make money and then return to the Punjab and farm for myself instead of on the ancestoral property."

Some of the migrants went to other parts of Asia before coming to America. As Sikh soldiers in the British army, many migrants had gone to China in 1900 to fight in the Boxer Rebellion, an uprising that pitted Chinese nationalists against foreign armies. During three years of military service, Puna Singh heard exciting stories about America. In 1906, when he was 18 years old, he went to the United States.

Other Indians had been recruited to work as policemen in the British colony of Hong Kong. "I was born in the Punjabi district of India and served on the police force in Hong Kong, China, for some years," Sucha Singh told an interviewer in 1924. "While I was in China several Hindus returned and reported on the ease with which they could make money in America and so I decided to go."

Generally the migrants were the second or youngest sons, sent out by their fathers to earn money to pay family debts and mortgages. They went abroad under the sponsorship of their families. Their decision to emigrate was not a solitary one, to fulfill their own desires or hopes, but a collective decision based on kinship duties and the family's needs.

To pay for their transportation to Vancouver or San Francisco, many Punjabis mortgaged one or two acres of their land in India. Even if they had to go into debt to get to America, they thought the promise of getting ahead by working in the new land was worth the sacrifice. They were paid only 10 or 15 cents a day in India, but they were told they could earn $2 for a day's work in America. A Sikh migrant later recalled how California seemed "enchanted."

Asian Indians at work picking crops in California. Of all the Asian groups who came to America in the first wave of migration, the Indians came in the smallest number: about 6,400. Nearly all of them had families in India.

Chinese schoolchildren in an American school, around 1890.
Although most of the Asian immigrants thought of themselves as
visitors, not permanent settlers, they soon began putting down roots.
Their children grew up thinking of America as home.

Chapter Seven

Pacific Passages

PUSHED FROM THEIR HOMELANDS AND PULLED TO America, the migrants left their families, friends, and loved ones in China, Japan, Korea, the Philippines, and India. There were many differences among the various groups that made up the first wave of Asian immigration. They ranged in numbers from approximately 430,000 Chinese, 380,000 Japanese, and 150,000 Filipinos to only about 8,000 Koreans and still fewer Asian Indians. They brought a rich variety of religions: Taoism, Buddhism, Shintoism, Hinduism, Islam, Sikhism, and Christianity. The groups differed in gender composition, too. Almost all of the Chinese, Filipino, and Asian-Indian migrants were men, but the Koreans and the Japanese included significant numbers of women. The men generally chose to come, but many of the women had no choice. Their husbands had decided for them, or they were brought to America as prostitutes. Most of the migrants in each group came as sojourners, planning to work in America briefly and then return to their homeland. But many others thought that perhaps they would stay. The number of permanent settlers increased among the Chinese after the Chinese Exclusion Act of 1882 and among the Japanese after the Gentlemen's Agreement of 1908. Entering through loopholes in these rules that were designed to keep them out, many Chinese and Japanese came to join family members and make their homes in America.

The migrants also came from different educational and social backgrounds. Most of the Japanese and Koreans could read and write, but most members of the other groups had very little schooling, or none at all. The Koreans came from cities; most of the others came from the countryside. The Chinese, coming from a country with a weak central government, lacked a strong sense of nationalism; in contrast, the Japanese embraced the patriotism of Meiji Japan. Because Japan had invaded their country, many Koreans felt a defensive nationalism.

But the differences among the migrants were less striking than their similarities. They were stirred by a common discontent, and they came searching for a new start. Poverty was painful, but hunger and want were not unique to the migrants, for the men and women who stayed home were also hungry and poor. The migrants were the dreamers. They imagined what they could do in America, and their dreams inspired them to take risks. They wondered what they could become, unfurled before the winds of change and challenge.

Possibilities exploded in their minds. They went to bed in the evenings with ideas and calculations roaring in their brains, and they woke up in the mornings shivering with excitement and restlessness. Visions of a brighter future swept them toward a break from their customs and homelands.

Ah, but the world is big, others warned them: Do you know the meaning of immensity? And they answered, We will tell you someday when we get back. The migrants felt their hearts tugging them toward America as they separated themselves from the graves of their ancestors and from a world where people looked like them and spoke their language.

Many of the migrants had never before stepped beyond the boundaries of their farm or village. Entering the port cities, they were confused and frightened by the noises and the crowds. At the docks, they said their final goodbyes. "When I departed Naha Harbor," a Japanese migrant remembered, "my mother sang loudly and danced with other women relatives until my ship went out of sight. Her song went like this: 'My beloved child, on this auspicious ship, may your journey be as safe and straight as if linked by a silk thread.'"

Another mother told her departing daughter, "I am going to miss you very much when you leave, but I'll always be with you. We won't be separated even for a moment." The daughter did not understand what her mother meant until that night. When she got ready for bed she found a piece of a Buddhist altar ornament tucked into her kimono. Waving goodbye to her mother, a young Filipina said she would be back in seven years. "But I knew," she told her granddaughter many years later, "I was never coming back."

After the goodbyes, there was a surge toward the moored ships, and the travelers began struggling through a sea of people. "Everyone was afraid that he would be left behind," said a Chinese migrant, "so as soon as the way was opened everyone just rushed to get on board and when he was finally aboard he was all out of breath."

The ship pulled away from the dock. As she felt her ship sail away from Yokohama, a Japanese woman watched the city disappear behind the waves. "The ship gained speed heartlessly out into the open sea," she said. "I could see nothing but water, when suddenly, and so unexpectedly, I sighted Mount Fuji poking its head above the horizon. I thought that Mount Fuji was stretching itself up to say, 'Goodbye,' to me. 'Ah! Fuji-san,' was all I could utter."

From the ships, Filipinos looked at pretty young women waving goodbye from the docks and giving them "remember me *manong*" smiles. A song captured the moment of farewell:

> You were still waving, beloved
> When I left you
> To journey to another land
> A white kerchief
> You held
> Drenched with tears
> You couldn't help crying
> I promised it'll be short
>   while perhaps
> And I will be back home. . . .

Gazing at the distant shores of Manila and holding his rattan suitcase, a *manong* felt a deep emptiness within. He recalled, "I knew that I was going away from everything I had loved and known. I waved my hat and went into the vestibule that led to the filthy hold below."

Nearly all of the migrants crossed the sea as steerage passengers—that is, they traveled in the least expensive, least comfortable quarters, below the decks at the rear of the ship. Steerage voyagers were packed together. "It was crowded below deck," a Filipina later recalled. "I think there were more than 300 of us; my husband was in a different section while the women and children were in another section. During the long voyage I would often sit on deck, holding my youngest child. . . . My husband and my other child, who was four, would often go and watch through the fence the first class passengers playing in the swimming pool."

The smell of freight, oil, and machines filled the air of the stifling steerage. The passengers tried to climb out onto the deck where they could breathe fresh air and see the sun, but "the first-class passengers were annoyed," a Filipino said, "and an official of the boat came down and drove us back into the dark haven below."

Their meals were terrible and monotonous. "The food was different from that which I had been used to, and I did not like it at all," a Chinese passenger complained. "When I got to San Francisco I was half starved because I was afraid to eat the provisions of the barbarians."

A Japanese traveler remembered that "the cooks and the ship's boys were Chinese, and every day we had curry rice only." Time and again Japanese passengers grumbled about the food. One said, "Breakfast and lunch consisted of bean paste soup and pickled radish. For supper we were served fatback. Though rice was served, it was so hard it wouldn't go down the throat. There was no soy sauce, and everything was literally awful."

A Filipino described the food of the steerage passengers on the steamship *President Pierce*: "wilted pechay (Chinese cabbage) and rotten vegetables; putrefied fish, salted pork, and stale hamburger for meats; and foul-smelling brew of tea and coffee made from sea water for drinks." Another Filipino traveler reported, "Food was served in great buckets." Filipinos were disappointed to find these buckets filled with bread rather than rice. They missed their daily rice, which one of them called "food which every hardworking Filipino cannot do without, especially in the morning."

Sometimes it did not matter what the passengers ate, for the seas were so rough that they became seasick and could not keep their food down. The world seemed to be in constant motion, swaying and rocking.

I ate wind and tasted waves for more than twenty days,

a Chinese traveler wrote in a poem he had carved on the walls of the Angel Island immigration station in San Francisco Bay. "Day after day the weather was bad and the sea stormy," a Japanese passenger said. "The hatch was tightly closed and there was no circulation of air, so we were all tortured by the bad odor." The passengers felt grimy, but they had no place to wash or bathe. On one ship, the crew put a long row of bowls on deck, filled half full of water for the passengers to rinse out their mouths and wash their faces.

Always the travelers faced the danger of epidemics sweeping through the steerages. On one occasion, 597 Chinese were forced to remain on their disease-infected ship for two months after it had reached Honolulu. A Filipino migrant never forgot the horror of a meningitis epidemic on board his ship: "The Chinese waiters stopped coming into our dining room, because so many of us had been attacked by the disease. They pushed the tin plates under the door of the kitchen and ran back to their rooms, afraid of being contaminated. Those hungry enough crawled miserably on their bellies and reached for their plates." Every now and then, he added, a young doctor and his assistant descended below deck to "check the number of deaths and to examine those about to die."

The steerage passengers slept on bunk beds in rows like those in an army barracks. Sleep did not come easily, due to the crowding, excitement, and anxiety. "I could not sleep a few nights," explained Choo-en Yang, who left Korea in 1902, "because so many things were in my mind and I worried so much since I did not know what would happen in the new, strange land in Hawaii. I did not know how to speak English

Immigrants at a detention center on Angel Island, near San Francisco, wait to be admitted to the United States. Many of them wrote poems on the center's walls. One poem reads: "Imprisoned in the wooden building day after day, My freedom withheld; how can I bear to talk about it?"

and I did not know anything about sugar plantation work either."

Japanese travelers tried to occupy themselves during the crossing by presenting traditional dramas and holding talent shows for singing, chanting poems, and playing the guitar. Passengers had time for reflection. As he lay on his bunk in the dark hole of the steerage, a Filipino traveler felt seasick and lonely. "I was restless at night," he said, "and many disturbing thoughts came to my mind." Perhaps he had made a mistake, but it was too late. He could not turn back now.

Theirs was a long, weary, and trying Pacific crossing. A Japanese voyager summed it up in a poem:

> *Island soul of me*
> *Cast off to cross the ocean.*
> *Ah, the world is big!*

The surging, swirling ocean around them seemed like the cresting and crashing of their emotions and thoughts.

They were in movement, with nothing solid and stable beneath them.

The migrants were awash with questions about their future: What would life be like in the new and foreign land, so far away? What would they become there? Would they ever see their homelands and families again? Would it be worth risking everything they had?

> *Loud waves rise and fall*
> *On the North Pacific sea*
> *Voyaging abroad*
> *I stand on froth-washed decks*
> *And am wet with salty spray.*

Finally, after four to eight weeks of confinement aboard ship, the tired and homesick passengers saw, on the distant horizon, the land of their destiny. That far-off speck of land grew larger and nearer. Soon the ship dropped anchor or tied up at a wharf, and dock workers began unloading the bales and crates of cargo. The travelers gathered their possessions and left the ship.

An observer described the arrival of Chinese passengers in San Francisco on the *Great Republic* in 1869. "Gazing in silent wonder at the new land," the Chinese were "packed" on the main deck. Then down the gangway they came, "a living stream of the blue-coated men of Asia," bending long bamboo poles across their shoulders to carry their bedding and clothing. They were dressed in new cotton blouses and loose baggy breeches, slippers or shoes with heavy wooden soles, and broad-brimmed hats of split bamboo. "For two mortal hours," the witness wrote, "the blue stream pours

Filipino workers bound for the Hawaiian sugar fields wore metal tags bearing the numbers assigned to them by the plantation owners.

down from the steamer upon the wharf; a regiment has landed already, and still they come."

The moment of arrival was engraved in the memories of the passengers. When Ch'ang-ho Ahn of Korea first saw the volcanic mountains of Hawaii rising from the sea, he was so deeply moved and overjoyed he later gave himself the pen name To San, meaning Island Mountain. A Filipino laborer named Bonipasyo described his arrival in Hawaii this way: "At 8 A.M. we pulled into the immigration station of Honolulu. There was a band playing. We disembarked alphabetically and as we came down the gangplank, they [the immigration officials] asked us where we were going and we shouted the plantation of our destiny. 'Waialua Sugar Company!' 'Puunene Maui!' people shouted. I shouted, 'Naalehu, Hawaii.'" Then Bonipasyo and his fellow Filipino laborers heard their names called. Each stepped forward, and a plantation official placed a *bango*, a numbered metal tag on a chain, around his neck.

Kin Huie, a Chinese from Guangdong, sighted California on "a clear, crisp, September morning in 1868" after a 60-day voyage. "To be actually at the 'Golden Gate' of the land of our dreams! The feeling that welled up in us was indescribable," he recalled. After Huie and the other passengers got off the boat, "out of the general babble, some one called out in our local dialect, and, like sheep recognizing the voice only, we blindly followed, and soon were piling into one of the waiting wagons. Everything was so strange and so exciting. . . . The wagon made its way heavily over the

Japanese picture brides receive vaccinations upon arriving in the United States. Their arrival was a blur of strange and often confusing new experiences.

cobblestones, turned some corners, ascended a steep climb, and stopped at a clubhouse, where we spent the night."

Arriving brides, married to men they had not yet met, felt a special sense of anticipation and anxiety. "A month after the marriage," a Chinese woman said, "I sailed for America with my husband's relative, a distant clan cousin." Her family had arranged her marriage to a man she had never seen. The ship docked at Port Townsend in Washington, and the cousin took the woman on deck. He pointed to a man walking up and down the wharf and said, "See that man smoking a big cigar? He is your husband!" A Japanese woman remembered how most of the passengers on her ship were picture brides: "When the boat anchored, one girl took out a picture from her kimono sleeve and said to me, 'Mrs. Inouye, will you let me know if you see this face?'" After arriving in San Francisco in 1919, Fusayo Fukuda was placed in a large waiting room with other picture brides. All the husbands came except hers. Panic swept through her as she looked around the empty room. She was wishing she could return to Japan when finally her husband, Yokichi Kaya, arrived.

Most of the picture brides were much younger than their husbands. "When I first saw my fiance, I could not believe my eyes," said Anna Choi, who was 15 years old when she became a picture bride. "His hair was grey and I could not see any resemblance to the picture I had. He was forty-six years old." Surprised and shocked to find older men waiting for them on the dock in Honolulu, many Korean picture brides cried, "Aigo omani!" ("Oh dear me, what shall I do?")

One of these startled picture brides was Hong Pong Yun Woo. Arriving in the islands at the age of 23, she saw a 36-year-old man greeting her as her new husband. "When I

see him," she said years later, "he skinny and black. I no like. No look like picture. But no can go home." Another Korean picture bride, finding that her prospective husband did not look like his picture, cried for eight days and refused to leave her room. "But I knew that if I don't get married, I have to go back to Korea on the next ship," she said. "So on the ninth day I came out and married him. But I don't talk to him for three months."

Wearing kimonos and sandals as they disembarked from the ships, Japanese picture brides often found themselves taken by their husbands straight to clothing stores and outfitted with Western dress. One young woman remembered putting on a high-collared blouse, a long skirt, high-laced shoes, and—for the first time in her life—a bra. She found her new underwear particularly baffling (Japanese women wore only sarong-like underskirts under their kimonos). "Wearing Western-style underwear for the first time, I would forget to take it down when I went to the toilet," she recalled. "And I frequently committed the blunder."

The migrants wondered how they would be received by Americans. Chinese newcomers asked apprehensively whether they would find themselves "eating bitterness" in the land of Gold Mountain. In China, they had been warned about the "red haired, green eyed" whites with "hairy faces." Now, in San Francisco, as they were driven through the streets in wagons, Chinese were often pelted with bricks thrown by white hoodlums. Finally, the tired and bruised travelers crossed Kearney Street and entered Chinatown, relieved to get away from the *fan gui* ("foreign devils"). They were glad to find "Chinese faces delighting the vision, and Chinese voices greeting the ear."

The experience of John Jeong showed what happened to many Chinese. After landing in San Francisco in 1900, he and several others were put in a carriage to be taken to Chinatown. "It was an open carriage with standing room only," recalled Jeong years later. "Halfway there some white boys came up and started throwing rocks at us. The driver was a white man, too, but he stopped the carriage and chased them away."

After a group of Japanese had arrived in San Francisco in 1905, they saw a gang of 20 white youngsters on the dock. "The Japs have come!" the youths shouted, and they threw horse dung. "I was baptized with horse dung," a newcomer commented later. "This was my very first impression of America."

When they landed in San Francisco in 1906, several Koreans saw a group of white men standing around the gangplank. "One guy stuck his foot out," one of the migrants said, "and kicked up my mother's skirt. He spit on my face, and I asked my father, 'Why did we come to such a place? I want to go home to Korea.'" A year later, a traveler from India reached Seattle, where he and his fellow Sikhs received "strange looks" as people peered at their turbans and beards and listened curiously to their language.

Shortly after she had arrived in California's San Joaquin Valley, a young Japanese bride stood alone in the darkness outside her house. "If I looked really hard I could see, faintly glowing in the distance, one tiny light," she said. "And over there, I could see another. And over there another. And I knew that that was where people lived. More than feeling *sabishii* [lonely], I felt *samui* [cold]. It was so lonely it was beyond loneliness. It was cold."

The migrants began to sense that they had crossed new boundaries, spiritual and cultural boundaries as well as

Allowed to leave Angel Island at last, immigrants board a ferry that will take them to San Francisco.

Carlos Bulosan came to America from the Philippines at the age of 17. During the Great Depression of the 1930s, he was a migrant farm worker. He became a writer, capturing the experiences of Filipinos in poems, essays, and stories.

geographical ones. They anxiously gathered memories around themselves. Filipino poet Carlos Bulosan wrote:

> *Alone I watch*
> *The world moving in space, looking back into*
> *Childhood for the words that meant so much,*
> *The voices that had gone with the years.*
> *This is the hour of memory.*

They tried to remember the familiar places they had left behind—their homes, the neighbor's fruit tree sagging with clusters of red *li-chi* fruit, the nearby stream where they caught shrimp with nets, the favorite footpath where delicious mountain bamboo shoots grew everywhere, and the secret places where they picked mushrooms. The farther they went from their village, the more vivid it became in their minds. "There are mountains on one side, and there is the wide river on the other side," said a migrant remembering his village. "A tongue of land extends into the river and on this land are hills that are covered with guava trees. Now is the time for the guavas to bloom. I used to go there when I was a child and the smell of the blossoms followed me down into the valley." A Japanese migrant spoke of:

> *Chasing them in dreams,*
> *Mountains and rivers of home.*

"Why had I left home?" a newcomer asked. "What would I do in America? I looked into the faces of my companions for a comforting answer, but they were as young and bewildered as I."

> *Illusion and I*
> *Travelled over the ocean*
> *Hunting money-trees.*
> *Looking and looking. . .*

> *Even in America*
> *What? No money-trees?*

And so the first wave of Asian migrants entered a new and alien world where they would become a racial minority, where they would be seen as different and inferior—where they would become "strangers from a different shore."

Chronology

1639	Japan's rulers isolate the country from the outside world.
1778	Captain James Cook of Britain is the first European to land in Hawaii.
1789	The first Chinese arrive in Hawaii as sailors.
1835	William Hooper of Boston comes to Kauai to start the first sugar plantation.
1836	The first Chinese are employed as plantation workers in Hawaii.
1839–42	China and Britain fight the first Opium War; China loses.
1848	California, once part of Mexico, becomes the property of the United States.
1849	The California gold rush begins; Chinese immigrants are among the "Forty-Niners" who flock to California to seek their fortunes.
1850	Sugar planters form the Royal Hawaiian Agricultural Society to bring laborers from China.
1853	Commodore Matthew C. Perry of the U.S. Navy forces Japan to open its doors to foreign trade.
1856–60	China and Britain fight the second Opium War; China loses.
1868	The Japanese emperor is restored to power, and the Meiji Era, a period of modernization, begins in Japan.
1875	The Reciprocity Treaty allows Hawaii to sell sugar to the United States without paying import taxes, boosting the sugar industry in the islands;

the Page Act limits the entry of Chinese women into the United States.

1882   The Chinese Exclusion Act is passed to keep Chinese laborers out of the United States.

1886   Large-scale Japanese immigration to Hawaii begins.

1888   The first Japanese laborers are brought to California.

1890s   Large-scale Japanese immigration to the United States begins.

1898   The United States takes possession of Hawaii and the Philippine Islands.

1900   Hawaii becomes a territory of the United States.

1904   Japanese troops invade Korea.

1906   Filipino immigration to Hawaii begins.

1907   Workers from India begin immigrating to the United States.

1908   In a treaty called the Gentlemen's Agreement, Japan agrees to limit the number of Japanese immigrating to the United States.

1910   Japan annexes Korea.

1914   Canada passes an immigration law limiting the number of emigrants from India.

1920   Large-scale Filipino immigration to the United States begins.

1921   Japan ends the practice of sending "picture brides" to the United States.

1924   The Immigration Act limits the number of people of each nationality who can move to the United States and prohibits the entry of immigrants from Asia.

Further Reading

Bulosan, Carlos. *America Is in the Heart: A Personal History.* Seattle: University of Washington Press, 1981.

Chan, Sucheng. *Asian Americans: An Interpretive History.* Boston: Twayne, 1991.

————. *This Bitter-Sweet Soil: The Chinese in American Agriculture, 1860–1910.* Berkeley: University of California Press, 1986.

Char, Tin-Yuke. *The Sandalwood Mountains: Readings and Stories of the Early Chinese in Hawaii.* Honolulu: University of Hawaii Press, 1975.

Chen, Jack. *The Chinese of America: From the Beginnings to the Present.* New York: Harper & Row, 1981.

Choy, Bong-Yuon. *Koreans in America.* Chicago: Nelson-Hall, 1977.

Cordova, Fred. *Filipinos—Forgotten Asian Americans: A Pictorial Essay.* Dubuque, IA: Kendall Hunt, 1983.

Daley, William. *The Chinese-Americans.* New York: Chelsea House, 1987.

Gee, Emma, ed. *Asian Women.* Berkeley: Asian American Studies, University of California, 1971.

Glick, Clarence. *Sojourners and Settlers: Chinese Immigrants in Hawaii.* Honolulu: University of Hawaii Press, 1980.

Golab, Caroline. *Immigrant Destinations.* Philadelphia: Temple University Press, 1977.

Hom, Marlon K., ed. and trans. *Songs of Gold Mountain: Cantonese Rhymes from San Francisco Chinatown.* Berkeley: University of California Press, 1987.

Ichioka, Yuji. *Issei: The World of the First-Generation Japanese Immigrants, 1885–1924*. New York: Free Press, 1988.

Inouye, Daniel. *Journey to Washington*. Englewood Cliffs, NJ: Prentice-Hall, 1967.

Ito, Kazuo, ed. *Issei: A History of Japanese Immigrants in North America*. Seattle, WA: Japanese Community Service, 1973.

Jensen, Joan M. *Passage from India: Asian Indian Immigrants in North America*. New Haven: Yale University Press, 1988.

Jones, Claire. *The Chinese in America*. Minneapolis: Lerner Publications, 1972.

Kikumura, Akemi. *Through Harsh Winters: The Life of a Japanese Immigrant Woman*. Novato, CA: Chandler & Sharp, 1981.

Kitano, Harry. *The Japanese-Americans*. New York: Chelsea House, 1988.

Knoll, Tricia. *Becoming Americans: Asian Sojourners, Immigrants, and Refugees in the Western United States*. Portland, OR: Coast to Coast Books, 1982.

Lai, Him Mark, Genny Lim, and Judy Yung, eds. *Island: Poetry and History of Chinese Immigrants on Angel Island*. San Francisco: Chinese Culture Foundation, 1980.

Leathers, Noel L. *The Japanese in America*. Minneapolis: Lerner Publications, 1991.

Lee, Joann Faung Jean. *Asian American Experiences in the U.S.: Oral Histories of First to Fourth Generation Americans from China, the Philippines, Japan, India, the Pacific Islands, Vietnam, and Cambodia*. Jefferson, NC: McFarland Press, 1991.

Lehrer, Brian. *The Korean-Americans*. New York: Chelsea House, 1988.

McCunn, Ruthanne Lum. *Thousand Pieces of Gold*. San Francisco: Design Enterprises, 1981.

Mayberry, Jodine. *Filipinos*. New York: Franklin Watts, 1990.

Melendy, Howard Brett. *Asians in America: Filipinos, Koreans, and East Indians*. New York: Hippocrene, 1981.

————. *The Oriental Americans*. Boston: Twayne, 1972.

Patterson, Wayne. *The Koreans in America*. Minneapolis: Lerner Publications, 1977.

Perrin, Linda. *Coming to America: Immigrants from the Far East*. New York: Delacorte, 1980.

Reimers, David M. *The Immigrant Experience*. New York: Chelsea House, 1989.

Stern, Jennifer. *The Filipino-Americans*. New York: Chelsea House, 1989.

Takaki, Ronald. *From Different Shores: Perspectives on Race and Ethnicity in America*. New York: Oxford University Press, 1987.

————. *Iron Cages: Race and Culture in Nineteenth-Century America*. New York: Knopf, 1979.

Wilson, Robert A., and Bill Hosokawa. *East to America: A History of the Japanese in the United States*. New York: Morrow, 1980.

Yung, Judy. *Chinese Women of America: A Pictorial History*. Seattle: University of Washington Press, 1986.

Index

The son of immigrant plantation laborers from Japan, **RONALD TAKAKI** graduated from the College of Wooster, Ohio, and earned his Ph.D. in history from the University of California at Berkeley, where he has served both as the chairperson and the graduate advisor of the Ethnic Studies program. Professor Takaki has lectured widely on issues relating to ethnic studies and multiculturalism in the United States, Japan, and the former Soviet Union and has won several important awards for his teaching efforts. He is the author of six books, including the highly acclaimed *Strangers from a Different Shore: A History of Asian Americans,* and the recently published *A Different Mirror: A History of Multicultural America.*

REBECCA STEFOFF is a writer and editor who has published more than 50 nonfiction books for young adults. Many of her books deal with geography and exploration, including the three-volume set *Extraordinary Explorers,* recently published by Oxford University Press. Stefoff also takes an active interest in environmental issues. She served as editorial director for two Chelsea House series—*Peoples and Places of the World* and *Let's Discover Canada.* Stefoff studied English at the University of Pennsylvania, where she taught for three years. She lives in Portland, Oregon.